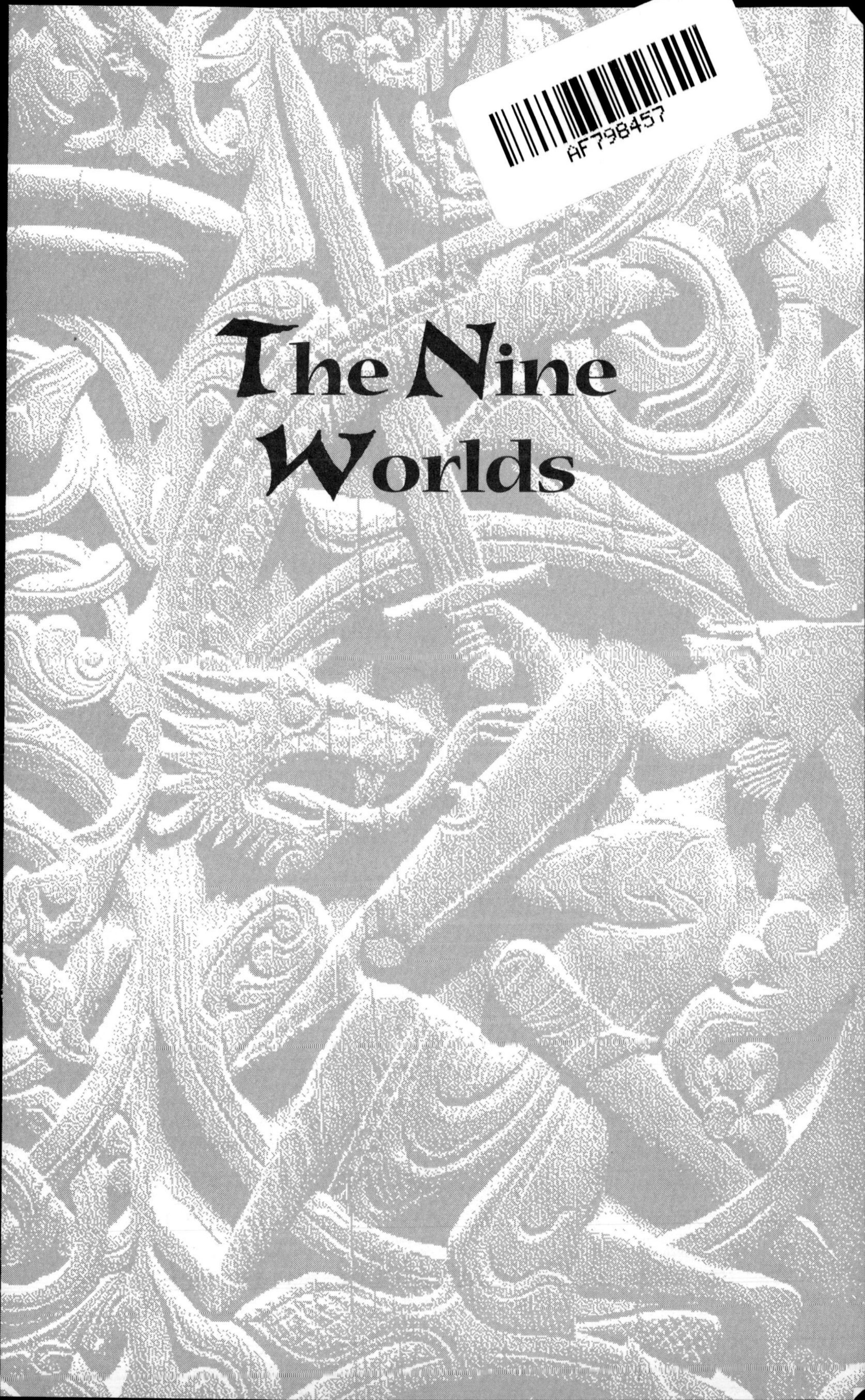

The Nine Worlds

"Dag" Rossman tales available on cassette
from Skandisk, Inc.:

Ice & Fire: Tales from Norse Mythology
Hammer & Mistletoe: Tales from Norse Mythology
Troll Tales
The Ring of Doom: The Saga of Sigurd
Wizard Ways

Cover photograph: Runestone marking the location of a ford at Ulunda, Uppland, Sweden, on Eriksgata—the ancient King's Road. Photo by "Dag" Rossman.

The Nine Worlds

A Dictionary of Norse Mythology

written by
Douglas "Dag" Rossman

illustrated by
Sharon Rossman

SKANDISK INC.

Skandisk, Inc., Bloomington, MN

Skandisk, Inc.
6667 West Old Shakopee Road, Suite 109
Bloomington, Minnesota 55438
www.tomten-skandisk.com

 First edition 1983 by Ormsgard Press
Second edition, revised and expanded © 2000 Skandisk, Inc.

Printed in the United States of America

Library of Congress Cataloging-in-Publication Data

Rossman, Douglas Athon, 1936-
The nine worlds : a dictionary of Norse mythology / written by Douglas "Dag" Rossman ; illustrated by Sharon Rossman.--2nd ed., rev. and expanded.
p. cm.
ISBN 1-57534-014-3 (alk. paper)
1. Mythology, Norse--Dictionaries. I. Title.

BL850 .R67 2000
293'.13'03--dc21 00-057376

The preface to this edition was previously published as "Ancient Nordic Spirituality: A Quest for Wisdom and Balance," *Scandinavian Press* (Fall 1996); reprinted in *Budstikken* (Dec. 1997).

Dedication

To all of our Norse ancestors—the historical, the legendary, and the mythological —this book is gratefully dedicated.
Mange tusen takk til vår forfedre.

Preface: Placing Norse Mythology in Context

In seeking to develop a personal philosophy that is both emotionally and intellectually satisfying, many of us shallow-rooted European-Americans have been drawn to the world views expressed by Native Americans or peoples of the Far East. Appealing as this approach may be, it is very difficult for most people to become completely attuned to a cultural heritage that is not their own. While one can respect and admire "the Other," most of us will always remain to some extent an outsider, a visitor in someone else's culture. The sense of truly belonging that we all crave continues to elude us.

Fortunately for people of Nordic descent, there is an ancient world view that is ours to claim by right of heritage—a philosophy as noble and earth-healing as those of the Far East or Native America. And it is not dead; it has only been forgotten for a time by many of its children. To begin recovering this world-view requires that we refamiliarize ourselves with Nordic mythology. The Norse myths are peopled with all sorts of fantastic beings—gods and giants, elves and dwarves, and, of course, dragons! But we must not make the mistake of taking these tales lightly. If we pay close attention to what the stories are saying we'll learn a great deal about what our ancestors thought was really important in life. . . and just what they felt it meant to be a human being. By exploring these myths we will come to better understand our ancestors and, hopefully, ourselves.

We must, of necessity, turn to mythology because the pre-Christian religion and religious practices did not long survive the Christianizing of northern Europe. True, some hints also have come down to us through folklore, but considering how the troll has been transformed from a terrifying monster into the cute Scandinavian mascot that it is today, one has to wonder about the accuracy of the surviving folklore images. This is not to suggest that the myths came through the Christianizing process unscathed. However, those that have survived were written down in the thirteenth century—a short enough period of time after the official conversion of Iceland (where most of them were recorded) that there was still an active poetic tradition that lent continuity to the beliefs of the past.

One of the two Icelandic sources of Nordic myths was the *Prose Edda* (or *Younger Edda*), written by Snorri Sturluson as a textbook to instruct budding skalds in the techniques and substance of skaldic poetry, using numerous myths as examples. Snorri was a Christian, but it is evident from his treatment of the mythic material that he retained an affectionate respect for the old stories and their characters.

The *Poetic Edda* (or *Elder Edda*) is a collection of 29 poems by various poets that was believed to have been assembled by an anonymous Icelandic compiler. Although not written down until later than the *Prose Edda*, internal evidence suggests that some of the poems go back at least into the Viking Age. Half of the poems deal with the myths of the gods, the other half with the legends of such folk heroes as Sigurd the Dragon Slayer.

There is also a Danish source from the same time period, the *Gesta Danorum* by Saxo Grammaticus, but Saxo's presentation of the stories is very different from those portrayed in the *Eddas* and today is generally not considered to be an accurate representation of the traditional myths.

What do the myths tell us about the ancient Nordic peoples' perception of their spiritual universe? That universe (or "multiverse," the term coined by Edred Thorsson in *Futhark: A Handbook of Rune Magic*) is organized into Nine Worlds interconnected and bound together by an immense ash tree called Yggdrasil (the World Tree). The Nine Worlds appear to be situated on three levels: an upper level includes Asgard, Vanaheim, and Alfheim; a middle level comprises Midgard, Jøtunheim, and Muspellheim; and a lower level includes Svartalfheim, Niflheim, and, presumably, Hel. Some scholars disagree about the placement of Muspellheim and question if Hel is a distinct realm or merely a part of Niflheim, but not to recognize Hel as separate raises the question as to what then would be considered the ninth world. Bifrost, the fiery rainbow bridge reaching from Asgard to Midgard, connects the upper and middle levels.

Different beings inhabit each of the Nine Worlds. In Asgard, there are the gods known as the Aesir; in Vanaheim, the Vanir gods; in Alfheim, the Light Elves; in Midgard, the humans; in Jötunheim, the Frost and Hill Giants; in Muspellheim, the Fire Giants; in Svartalfheim, the dwarves—the so-called Dark Elves; in Hel, the dead. There are few inhabitants in Niflheim, a land of cold and mist.

A gigantic root of the World Tree extends into each of

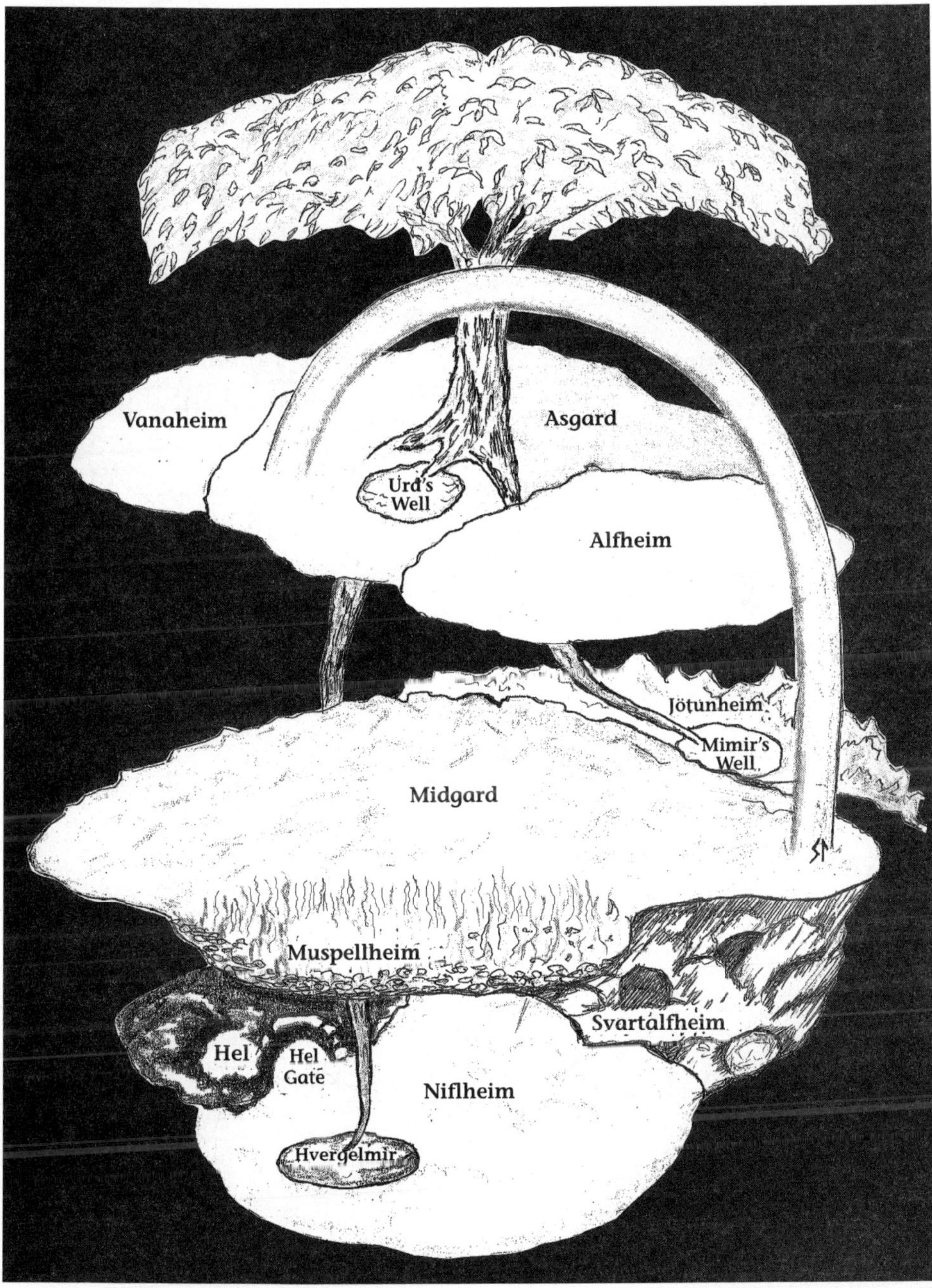

Yggdrasil, the World Tree, unites the Nine Worlds.

the three levels, and a great well or spring lies beneath each root—Hvergelmir in Niflheim, Mimir's Well in Jötunheim, and Urd's Well in Asgard. As we shall see later, Hvergelmir contains the water of creation, Mimir's Well the water of wisdom, and Urd's Well the water of healing for the World Tree.

How did these complex and marvelous worlds come into being? Two of them, Muspellheim (the land of fire) and Niflheim (the land of ice), apparently always existed, and between them lay a silent void called Ginnungagap. Poisonous, slushy, rime ice formed on the rivers pouring forth from the great spring Hvergelmir in Niflheim, flowed out into Ginnungagap, and came in contact with sparks and embers hurled into space by the volcanoes of Muspellheim. Soon the ice began to melt. From that dripping meltwater formed the enormous, sleeping giant Ymir. While he slept, the sweat gathering beneath his left armpit took the form of a male and a female and, at the same time, his feet mated with each other—in some totally unexplainable manner—to produce a son. Thus, the race of Frost Giants was created.

During this time—if time even existed then—the giant Ymir was sustained by milk dripping from the teats of the cosmic cow, Audumla, who also had formed from the melting ice. She, in turn, found nourishment by licking the salty blocks of ice. In so doing, she revealed a male figure who, after three days, stepped forth from the ice. He was called Buri and later became the grandfather of the first Aesir gods. His son Bor married the giantess Bestla and fathered three sons: Odin, Vili, and Ve—the first Aesir.

The three brothers fell upon the sleeping Ymir and killed him. So much blood flowed from his wounds that all of the Frost Giants drowned except for one family that managed to float to safety, thus saving their race from extinction. Odin and his brothers proceeded to dismember Ymir's body and create from it most of the rest of the Nine Worlds. From his flesh they made the land, from his bones the mountains, from his teeth the rocks and pebbles, from his blood the sea and lakes, from his hair the trees, from his skull the vault of the sky (held up by four dwarves, created from the maggots feeding on Ymir's corpse), from his brains the clouds, and from his eyebrows a barrier to separate Midgard from the lands of the giants. Then the three Aesir took the sparks from Muspellheim and cast them into the sky to form the sun, moon, and stars. At some point, four charioteers were appointed to ride across the sky, guiding the night, the day, the moon, and the sun.

Odin and his brothers then paused to survey their handiwork. Strolling along the shore one day, they came upon two trees, an ash and an elm, which they caused to take on the forms of a man and a woman, respectively. The gods breathed life into Ask and Embla, gave them wits and spirit, and granted them Midgard for themselves and their descendents—the human race. Then, high above it all, the Aesir created their own homeland, the magnificent realm of Asgard. It is interesting to note that in the Nordic world view the universe represents more of a transformation of previously existing matter than a creation from nothing, and the gods themselves are early products of that transformation rather than its prime initiators. Moreover, as we shall see, while Odin is regarded as the King of the Gods, unlike the Christian deity he is neither all-knowing nor all-powerful.

But all is not well in the Nine Worlds. The seeds of destruction seem to have been present in their creation from Ymir's corpse. One of those seeds is the constant hostility between the gods and their allies on the one hand, and the giants and trolls on the other. The giants are determined to eventually overthrow and destroy the gods—a task in which they will be aided by the treacherous Loki and his monster sons, Fenrir (or Fenris) Wolf and Jörmungand, the Midgard (or World) Serpent. Much of what takes place in the myths reflects this menace and the sense of a slow, unavoidable movement toward the final, universe-shattering confrontation (called Ragnarök, the Doom of the Gods) from which there will emerge no victor and few survivors.

Meanwhile, the World Tree, which binds together the fabric of the Nine Worlds and on whose survival their very existence depends, is under constant attack from all sides. A twining of serpents (or dragons—the ancient Norse made little distinction between them) lurks in Hvergelmir and gnaws at the root that lies in Niflheim. Four deer and a goat live on the limbs of Yggdrasil and eat its leaves, and the trunk of the Tree is infected with some sort of rot. Fortunately, however, each day healing water from Urd's Well is applied to the trunk of Yggdrasil by the three Norns—wise women (possibly of giant stock) who live near the Well. Thus is maintained the eternal balance between growth and decay.

Who are these Norns—these caretakers of the created order—and what is the symbolic significance of the Well and the Tree? Much of the following discussion is based on the thought-provoking ideas presented by Paul Bauschatz in *The Well and the Tree,* a book deserving careful exploration by the interested reader. The three Norns are called Urd, Verdandi, and Skuld, names that usually have been translated as Past, Present, and Future. Currently, however, most mythologists believe that Urd means Fate, referring to those actions that have already taken place; Verdandi means Becoming, referring to those actions in the process of taking place; and Skuld means Necessity, referring to those necessary actions that drive the whole process.

Each day as the Norns apply the healing water to Yggdrasil's trunk, they speak (or chant) the ørlög—the essential and unchanging laws of the universe that both drive and limit the events presently taking place in our world. Nowhere are we told precisely what the ørlög contains, but after much reading and meditation I would like to offer the following poem as an educated guess as to what lies at the heart of the ørlög.

ØRLÖG (THE NORNS' CHANT)

In the midst of darkness, light;
In the midst of death, life;
In the midst of chaos, order.

In the midst of order, chaos;
In the midst of life, death;
In the midst of light, darkness.

Thus has it ever been,
Thus is it now, and
Thus shall it always be.

The Norns' action is not merely a symbolic acknowledgment of significant past events; it is meant to create and empower the present—in a manner comparable, perhaps, to the restoration and revitalization of the Deamtime by Australian Aborigine elders when they chant the Songlines. The past is not seen as something remote, inaccessible, and fading away—rather it is growing ever larger and more powerful as more events occur and more knowledge is accumulated.

If the Well is seen as a repository of the past, the Tree represents the present, depending upon the water of the Well both for growth and healing. Thus the present is constantly influenced by all that has gone before. This active "power of the past upon the present" is sometimes referred to as *wyrd*. And, of course, the relationship between the Well and the Tree is reciprocal: once present events have taken place, their effects and implications drip like dew from the Tree back into the Well to enlarge the past and further complicate and/or clarify it.

Just to survive in this world, let alone live in such a way as to be favorably remembered after death, the wise person must learn as much as possible about the realms of the Well and the Tree. Thus he will come to glimpse—however dimly—the nature of wyrd itself, and to align himself with it. In doing so, he will also contribute to maintaining the universal balance embodied in the ørlög.

This myth-driven quest for knowledge of world and self may well have contributed to the significant involvement of the Nordic peoples in exploration, natural history, physical science, philosophy, and psychology. Such a quest demands great personal sacrifice, however, and is doomed to fall short of total enlightenment. After all, neither Odin's nine nights of suffering on the World Tree (hanging, spear-wounded, as a sacrifice to himself)—which won him the secrets of the runes—nor his sacrifice of an eye at Mimir's Well to gain a drink of the water of wisdom brought the King of the Gods full knowledge and understanding of the Nine Worlds.

No treatment of ancient Nordic spirituality would be

complete without at least a mention of the runes, letters carved on wood, bone, stone, or metal that not only served as part of a functional alphabet, but also symbolized key mythical-psychological concepts in the Nordic world view. Their importance cannot be overemphasized, as evidenced by Odin's aforementioned ordeal to learn their secrets. His self-sacrifice on the Tree was nothing less than a shamanic experience—a sort of Nordic vision quest in which he obtained the power inherent in the magical letters rather than the guidance of spirit guardians, as a Native American shaman might have done. Still, our Viking Age ancestors did believe in the existence of a personal *fylgja* (literally a "follower") that took the form of an animal or perhaps a humanlike spirit of the opposite gender. The fylgja usually could only be seen in dreams, by someone gifted with "second sight," or near the moment of death. Some mythologists have argued that Odin's ravens, Hugin and Munin (Thought and Memory), who bring him news about the Nine Worlds each day, are actually his fylgjur.

Closely associated in the Nordic mind with the runes, the Well, and the Tree, was the dragon. It is the most frequently encountered animal figure in the art of the Viking Age, including that appearing on the runestones. There the dragon's body usually contains the runes, not only artistically but symbolically, thus incorporating the knowledge and power that the runes themselves embody. Small wonder, then, that Sigurd could understand the language of birds after just a small taste of the dragon Fafnir's blood.

We have already noted that dragons are present in Hvergelmir, the well of creation, where they gnaw at one of Yggdrasil's roots. Another dragon we must consider is Jörmungand, the Midgard Serpent and Thor's greatest enemy, who encircles the world and grasps his tail in his mouth. It seems likely that he is the dragon represented on so many runestones, since that dragon often encircles a central figure that has been referred to as a "cross" but which has roots and supports eight vanes radiating from a central ring—surely a stylized representation of the World Tree supporting the Nine Worlds.

So, what is going on here? Why does a dragon, a presumably "evil" creature (after all, Jörmungand is fated to slay Thor at Ragnarök, and other dragons are gnawing on Yggdrasil each day), appear so frequently in conjunction with such a powerful symbol of "good" as the World Tree? It could be that the ancient Nordic philosophers were not so much concerned with passing judgement on what is good and what is evil as they were with expressing their understanding of "the way things are." Thus, the symbolic pairing of the Dragon (darkness, death, chaos) with the Tree (light, life, order) was in recognition—and acceptance—of the eternal balance of opposites. That acceptance is not always easy for an individual human heart to accomplish, but to seek anything other than the continuing balance of opposites would be to deny reality; and our Nordic ancestors were nothing if not clear-eyed realists, even in their myths.

Fortunately, when facing the reality that life can be awfully tough, our Nordic ancestors managed to elude the clutches of grim resignation or utter despair by aspiring to take on the attributes of the Nordic hero as embodied in the *drengskapur* (truthfulness, helpfulness, loyalty, fortitude, courage, self-respect, self-determination, self-reliance, self-restraint—see page 112), a choice available to everyone, not just warriors. By striving for personal excellence, one need not defeat life's foes in a physical, secular sense in order to have a meaningful existence.

It was not a philosophy of grim fatalism that our ancestors embraced (although some writers have stated that it was). The Nordic hero cherished existence and knew how to enjoy life, but he also could face death with a calm mind and a smile. No matter what happened, a hero could choose to behave with honor. "It matters not if you win or lose, but how you play the game" could well be the modern paraphrase of an old Nordic saying such as the following verse from the "Havamal" (Words of the High One) attributed to Odin:

Cattle die, kindred die,
Every man is mortal.
But the good name will never fade
Of one who has lived honorably.

Douglas "Dag" Rossman
"Ormsgard"
Decorah, Iowa
June 2000

Introduction

The purpose of this book is to provide an annotated list of the principal mythological beings, places, and magical implements mentioned in the *Eddas*. Although I have included the names of all the dwarves who are mentioned or listed, I have largely omitted the names of giants and giantesses that are merely listed in the *Prose Edda* without being associated with any story. There is ample precedent for this decision; both the Brodeur and the Young editions of the *Prose Edda*—my principal sources for that text—chose to omit the list of giant names as well. For the most part, I have also omitted semi-historical humans except for a very few, such as Sigurd, whose lives were directly and significantly involved with purely mythological figures. Thus I have undoubtedly included or excluded certain individuals another author might have treated differently. This simply reflects a matter of personal taste.

My perspective is not that of a scholar of mythology, but rather that of a storyteller who has been attracted to the power, the tragedy, and, yes, the humor of the Norse myths. I find they strike a deep, responsive chord in me; whether this appeal reflects nostalgic recognition of half-forgotten stories read in childhood or some racial memory welling up from the Scandinavian part of my ancestry, I cannot say nor do I think it really matters. I love these tales and I offer this little dictionary as an aid to others who share that same affection.

This list is more extensive than any accompanying the various books on Viking Age mythology published in America. However, it is not as exhaustive as the more scholarly *Dictionary of Northern Mythology* by Rudolf Simek (1984, D.S. Brewer, Cambridge, U. K.) and *Dictionary of Norse Myth and Legend* by Andy Orchard (1997, Cassell, London, U.K.). These books cover not only the *Eddas* but also the Icelandic sagas, as well as material from other Germanic cultures.

Although the *Eddas* were written in Old Norse, I have chosen to present the names with their more familiar English spellings. In doing so, I usually have omitted the terminal *r* and converted ð to *d* and þ to *th*. Where there are alternate spellings, in most cases I have followed the usage in the *Prose Edda*. In attempting to pronounce the names, the reader should remember that *j* sounds like the *y* in "yes," *ae* like the *a* in "man," *ei* like "aye," and *a* somewhat like "ah."

The translations I drew upon in compiling this dictionary are as follows:

Bellows, Henry A. 1923. *The Poetic Edda*. American Scandinavian Foundation, New York.

Brodeur, Arthur G. 1916. *The Prose Edda.* American Scandinavian Foundation, New York.

Hollander, Lee M. 1962. *The Poetic Edda.* University of Texas Press, Austin.

Taylor, Paul B., and W. H. Auden. 1967. *The Elder Edda: A Selection.* Vintage Books, New York.

Young, Jean I. 1954. *The Prose Edda of Snorri Sturluson: Tales from Norse Mythology.* University of California Press, Berkeley.

The best source of Norse myths currently available is the excellent collection of retold stories (with extensive commentaries and bibliography) published as part of the Pantheon Fairy Tale and Folklore Library:

Crossley-Holland, Kevin. 1980. *The Norse Myths.* Pantheon Books, New York.

Dictionary of Norse Mythology

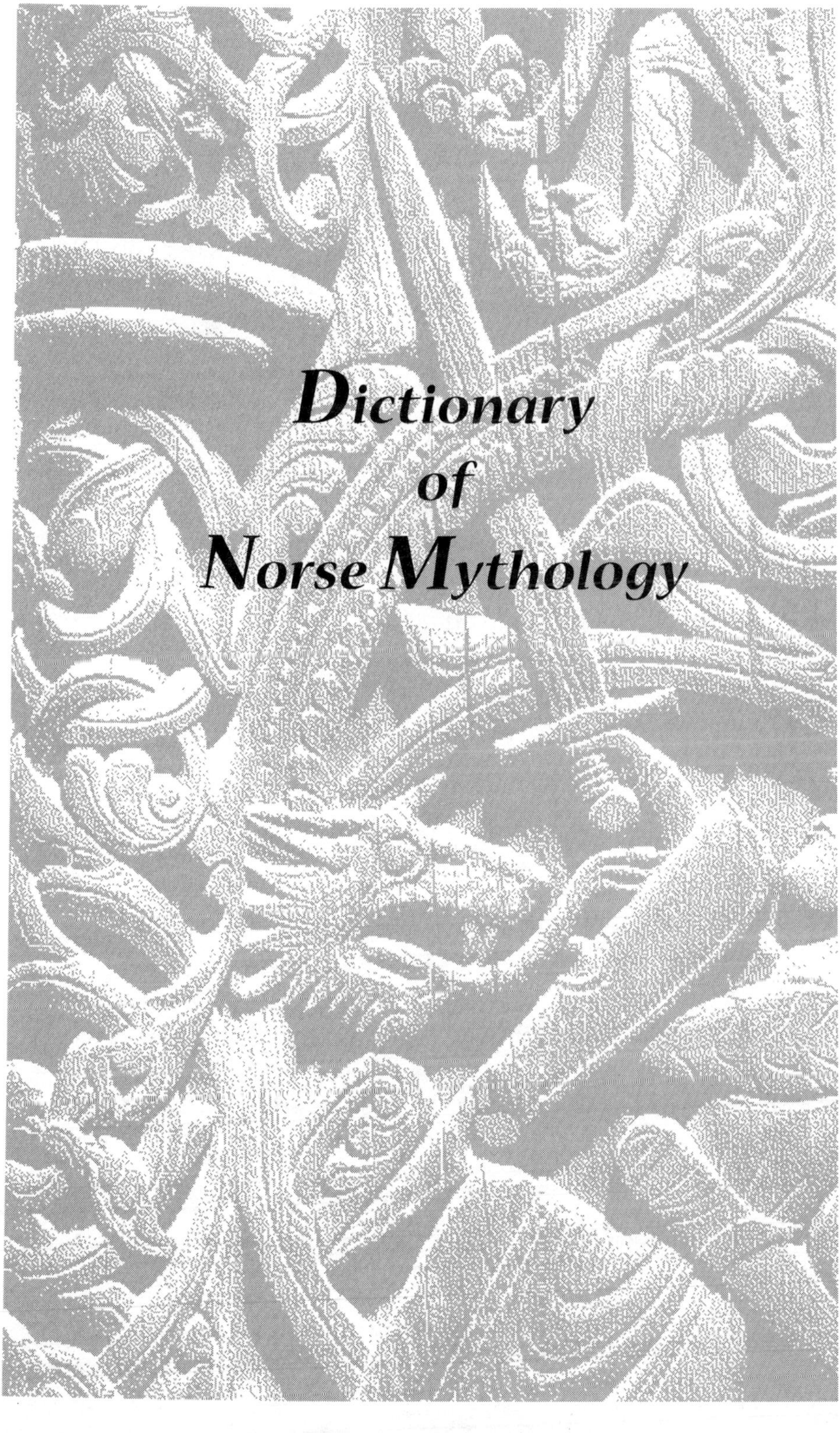

A

AEGIR. A giant and sea god; the son of the giant Mistarblindi and husband of Ran. He brews the Aesir's ale in his gold-lighted banquet hall on the island called Hlesey.

AEKIN. See EIKIN.

AESIR (singular, AS). One of the two races of Norse gods. The term usually is applied to Odin and his male descendents or kin. They live in Asgard.

AFI. The husband of Amma.

AGNAR. The elder son of King Hrauding who, at the instigation of Odin, was marooned by his younger brother, Geirröd.

AGNAR. The son of Geirröd and nephew of Agnar. He took mercy on Odin when, in the guise of Grimnir, the god was being tortured by Geirröd. Agnar succeeded his father to the kingship after Geirröd's untimely demise.

AI. The husband of Edda.

AI. One of the dwarves of Dvalin's band, which left the rocks to settle on a sandy plain.

ALF. One of the dwarves of Dvalin's band, which left the rocks to settle on a sandy plain.

ALFADIR. A nickname, or title, of Odin.

ALFAR (singular, ALF). The elves: when used without a descriptive adjective this term almost always refers to the Light Elves, who live in Alfheim. They are described as being fairer than the sun to look upon and are closely associated with the Aesir. Despite the fact that the Eddas frequently refer to them collectively, almost no elves are mentioned by name.

ALFHEIM. The part of Asgard where the Light Elves dwell. The gods presented it to Frey as a tooth-gift (a present given to a child when it cuts its first tooth).

ALFROTHUL. A nickname for the sun.

ALGRÖN. An island on which Odin dwelled with Fjölvar for five years.

ALI. See VALI.

ALSVID. A giant wise in rune lore. He gave the knowledge of runes to giantkind.

ALSVID. One of the two horses that pull the chariot of the sun across the heavens. See also ARVAK.

ALTHJOF. A dwarf.

ALVALDI. A giant; the father of Thjazi, Idi, and Gang. He was rich in gold.

ALVIS. A dwarf who somehow induced the Aesir to promise him Thor's daughter as a bride. Thor, who was not present when the pledge was made, engaged Alvis in a lengthy question-and-answer session, which ended with the rising of the sun and the dwarf turning to stone—a fate otherwise known to happen only to trolls.

AMLODI'S CHURN. A nickname for the sea. There are no clues to the identity of Amlodi, but the churn may refer to the magic mill Grotti.

AMMA. The wife of Afi and mother of Karl (by Rig).

AMSVARTNIR. The lake on which lies the island of Lyngvi where Fenrir is bound.

AN. A dwarf.

ANDHRIMNIR. The cook in Valhalla.

ANDLANG. The second level of the heavens, which lies to the south and above Asgard. See also ASGARD and VIDBLAIN.

ANDVARANAUT. The gold ring stolen from the dwarf Andvari by Loki as a part of Oter's weregild (compensation, or blood-price). The ring has carried Andvari's curse with it from that time forward.

ANDVARI. A dwarf; the son of Oin. He was the owner of a golden hoard stolen by Loki to pay Oter's weregild. Loki wouldn't even let Andvari keep one magic ring with which he could again become wealthy, so Andvari put a curse on the ring that it would destroy whomever possessed it. Andvari has the ability to transform himself into the form of a fish.

ANGEYA. A giantess; one of the nine sisters who mothered Heimdall.

ANGRBODA. A giantess; the mother (by Loki) of Fenrir, Jörmungand, and Hel. She lived in Jötunheim.

ANNAR. The second husband of the giantess Nott and father of Jörd. Also known as Onar.

ARVAK. One of the two horses that pull the chariot of the sun across the heavens. See also ALSVID.

ASA-THOR. A nickname of Thor.

ASGARD. The lowest level of the heavens or, more specifically, the stronghold of the Aesir that is located there. It is connected to Midgard by the rainbow bridge, Bifröst. See also ANDLANG and VIDBLAIN.

ASK. The first man, who was created from a tree (presumably an ash) by Bor's sons. He was the husband of Embla.

ASYNJUR (singular, ASYNJA). The female counterparts of the Aesir.

ATLA. A giantess; one of the nine sisters who mothered Heimdall.

ATRID. A nickname of Odin.

AUD. The son of the giantess Nott and her first husband, Naglfari.

AUDUMLA. The cow formed from the thawing frost in Ginnungagap. The four rivers of milk that flowed from her teats fed the giant Ymir. For nourishment she licked the salty blocks of ice and, in the course of three days, there appeared from the ice-blocks Buri, the ancestor of the Aesir.

AURBODA. A giantess; the wife of the giant Gymir. Their daughter, Gerd, is the fairest of all women.

AURBODA. One of the nine handmaidens of Menglod. It is possible that she and the giantess Aurboda may be the same person.

AURGELMIR. The Frost Giants' name for Ymir.

AURNIR. A giant; apparently an uncle of Fenja or Menja, or both.

AURVANDIL. The first (?) husband of the seeress Groa and (according to Branston, 1955, *Gods of the North*) first husband of Sif, by whom he fathered Ull. He was carried out of Jötunheim over the Elivagar in a basket by Thor, who waded the icy streams. One of Aurvandil's toes had stuck out of the basket and frozen solid. Thor broke it off and hurled it into the sky where it remains to this day as the star called Aurvandil's Toe (which Grimm, 1875-78, *Deutsche Mythologie,* thought actually might be the planet Venus). Branston also referred to Aurvandil as being an archer.

AURVANG. A dwarf.

AURVANGAR. The place in Jöruvellir to which the dwarves from Svarinshaug came. These localities presumably are associated with the migration of Dvalin's band.

AUSTRI. A dwarf; one of the four who hold up Ymir's skull (i.e., the sky). See also NORDRI, SUDRI, and VESTRI.

B

BAFUR. See BOFUR.

BALDER. One of the Aesir; a son of Odin and Frigg, the husband of Nanna, and father of Forseti. Frequently referred to as Balder the Beautiful or Balder the Good, he was said to be the best, the wisest, and the most eloquent of the gods. His death by the hand of his blind brother, Höd, which was arranged through the connivance and malice of Loki, initiated the chain of events leading inexorably to Ragnarök.

BALEYG. A nickname of Odin.

BARI. One of the nine dwarves who constructed the hall called Lyr where Menglod dwelled.

BARRI. The forest where Frey and Gerd met to consummate their love.

BAUGI. A giant; a son of Gilling and brother of Suttung. Odin tricked him into helping the god steal Suttung's Mead.

BELI. A giant whom Frey fought and slew with a stag's antler, his sword having been given to Skirnir.

BERGELMIR. A giant; the son of Thrudgelmir and grandson of Ymir. He and his wife were the only Frost Giants to survive the great flood caused by the blood flowing from Ymir's wounds when Bor's sons slew him. Thus Bergelmir and his wife are the ancestors of all the race of Frost Giants.

BESTLA. A giantess; the daughter of Bölthorn, sister of Mimir, wife of Bor, and mother of Odin, Vili, and Ve.

BEYLA. The wife of Byggvir and servant of Frey.

BIFLINDI. A nickname of Odin.

BIFRÖST. The fiery rainbow bridge that connects Asgard to Midgard. The fire keeps the Hill Giants and Frost Giants from entering Asgard. At Ragnarök the bridge will break beneath the hosts of Muspellheim. Bifröst is also referred to as the Gjallar Bridge or Windhelm's Bridge.

BIFUR. A dwarf.

BIL. One of the Asynjur; the sister of Hjuki. She and her brother are the two children who follow Mani through the heavens as he guides the course of the moon. He took them from the earth when they were bearing water from the well Byrgir. Hjuki and Bil were the original "Jack and Jill."

BILD. A dwarf.

BILEYG. A nickname of Odin.

BILLING. The father of a maiden who flirted with Odin but ultimately denied him her sexual favors.

BILLING. A dwarf.

BILSKIRNIR. Thor's hall in Asgard. The largest house in all the worlds, it has 540 rooms.

BJORT. One of the nine handmaidens of Menglod.

BLAIN. The giant from whose bones the race of dwarves was made. This probably is a nickname of Ymir.

BLEIK. One of the nine handmaidens of Menglod.

BLID. One of the nine handmaidens of Menglod.

BLODUGHADDA. One of the nine daughters of Aegir and Ran.

BLODUGHOFI. A horse said to have been ridden by Odin and Frey.

BODN. One of the two vats used by Fjalar and Galar to collect Kvasir's blood. See also SON and ODRÖRIR.

BODVILD. The daughter of Nidud. She was either seduced or raped by Völund in revenge for her father's mistreatment of the smith. According to *Thidrek's Saga* she subsequently bore a son named Vidga.

BOFUR. A dwarf.

BOR. The son of Buri, husband of Bestla, and father of Odin, Vili, and Ve.

BÖLTHORN. A giant; the father of Bestla—and probably Mimir—and grandfather of Odin, Vili, and Ve.

BÖLVERK. A nickname of Odin, the one he used on his quest for Kvasir's blood.

BÖMBUR. A dwarf.

BRAGI. The Aesir god of poetry; the husband of the goddess Idun and, presumably, son of Odin and

Gunnlöd. He is renowned for his wisdom and eloquence.

BREIDABLIK. Balder's beautiful dwelling in Asgard.

BRIMIR. The giant from whose blood (along with Blain's bones) the gods made the dwarves. This is probably a nickname for Ymir.

BRIMIR. According to the Prose Edda, a hall in Okolnir that will serve as a refuge for men in the afterlife. However, the *Poetic Edda* says that it is Brimir's hall, rather than a hall called Brimir, which is in Okolnir.

BRIMIR. The name of the sword carried by Odin according to Hollander's translation of the *Poetic Edda*. According to Bellow's translation, however, Odin had Brimir's sword rather than a sword called Brimir.

BRISINGAMEN. Freyja's necklace, which was fashioned by four dwarves: Alfrigg, Berling, Dvalin, and Grerr (their names are not mentioned in this context in the *Eddas* but come from the later *Sorla Thattr*). According to a non-Eddic source, *Tale of Hogni and Hedinn*, Freyja purchased the necklace by granting the dwarves her sexual favors.

BROKK. A dwarf; the brother of Eitri. He wagered with Loki that Eitri could make three gifts for the Aesir more precious than those made by Ivaldi's sons. When Loki tried to welsh on his bet, Brokk sewed his lips together with a thong.

BRUNI. A dwarf.

BRUNNAK'S BROOKLET. A small stream associated with Idun.

BURI. The first ancestor of the Aesir; the father of Bor and grandfather of Odin, Vili, and Ve. He was formed over a period of three days from ice blocks that were licked by the cow Audumla.

BURI. A dwarf.

BUSEYRA. A giantess whose blood was spilled by Thor.

BYGGVIR. The husband of Beyla and the servant of Frey.

BYLEIST. A giant; a son of Farbauti and Laufey, and brother of Loki and Helblindi.

BYLGJA. One of the nine daughters of Aegir and Ran.

BYRGIR. The well or spring from which Bil and Hjuki were drawing water when Mani took them into the heavens with him.

D

DAG. A son of the giantess Nott and the As Delling. He is radiant and fair like his father. Dag and his mother ride chariots through the heavens as they circle the world each day. Dag is a personification of day.

DAIN. One of the two dwarf smiths who fashioned Freyja's golden-bristled boar, Hildisvinni. See also NABBI.

DAIN. The elf who gave the knowledge of runes to elvenkind.

DAIN. One of the four stags that live in the branches of the ash Yggdrasil and eat its leaves. See also DUNEYR, DVALIN, and DYRATHRÖR.

DARK ELVES. See SVARTALFAR.

DARRI. One of the nine dwarves who constructed the hall called Lyr where Menglod dwelled.

DELLING. One of the Aesir; the third husband of the giantess Nott and father of Dag.

DELLING. One of the nine dwarves who constructed the hall called Lyr where Menglod dwelled.

DOLGTHRASIR. One of the dwarves in Dvalin's band, which left the rocks to settle on a sandy plain.

DOLGTHVARI. The name applied to the dwarf Dolgthrasir in the *Prose Edda.*

DORI. One of the nine dwarves who constructed the hall called Lyr where Menglod dwelled. He was also one of Dvalin's band, which left the rocks to settle on a sandy plain.

DRAUPNIR. The magic ring forged by the dwarf Eitri and presented to Odin. Every ninth night it produces eight other gold rings of equal weight. Odin laid the ring on Balder's funeral pyre, but it was sent back to Odin from Niflheim as a remembrance.

DRAUPNIR. One of the dwarves in Dvalin's band, which left the rocks to settle on a sandy plain.

DROMI. The second fetter (half again as strong as the first) that was placed on the great wolf Fenrir. With considerable effort he managed to break it, too. See also GLEIPNIR and LAEDING.

DRÖFN. One of the nine daughters of Aegir and Ran.

DUF. One of the dwarves in Dvalin's band, which left the rocks to settle on a sandy plain.

DUFA. One of the nine daughters of Aegir and Ran.

DUNEYR. One of the four stags that live in the branches of the ash Yggdrasil and eat its leaves. See also DAIN, DVALIN, and DYRATHRÖR.

DURIN. The second most prestigious leader of the race of dwarves.

DVALIN. One of the four stags that live in the branches of the ash Yggdrasil and eat its leaves. See also DAIN, DUNEYR, and DYRATHRÖR.

DVALIN. A major leader among the dwarves, he brought the knowledge of runes to the dwarvish race. The sun is called "Dvalin's Doom" by the dwarves, alluding to the fact that sunlight is harmful to them (his nickname, Solblindi, may give us a clue to the nature of

Dvalin leads his band of dwarves.

that harm). Some of the lesser norns are said to be "Dvalin's daughters," but in that context his name may be serving simply to represent dwarves generally.

DVALIN'S BAND. A group of dwarves who, under the leadership of Dvalin, left the rocks and settled on a sandy plain. Presumably those are the same dwarves who migrated from Svarinshaug to Aurvangar in Jöruvellir. They included Alf, Ali, Andvari, Dolgthrasir, Dori, Draupnir, Duf, Eikinskjaldi, Fid, Fjalar, Frosti, Ginnar, Gloin, Haugspori, Hlevang, Hör, Ori, Skafid, Skirvir, Virvir, and Yngvi.

DYRATHRÖR. One of the four stags that live in the branches of the ash Yggdrasil and eat its leaves. See also DAIN, DUNEYR, and DVALIN.

E

EDDA. The wife of Ai and mother of Thrall (by Rig).

EGGTHER. The joyous watchman of the giants, and guardian of the giantess of the Iron Wood. He sits upon a grave mound beneath a gallows tree and plays a harp. The cock Fjalar sits in the branches above him.

EGIL. The farmer who gave his son, Thjalfi, and daughter, Röskva, to Thor as servants to compensate the god for Thjalfi's unintentionally crippling one of Thor's goats.

EGIL. The brother of Völund and Slagfid, and husband of the valkyrie Olrun. They lived in Ulfdalir. When, in the ninth year, Olrun and her sister valkyries flew off through Myrkvid to the wars, Egil fared eastward to hunt for her. Since Völund is addressed as "elflord" by Nidud, presumably Egil is also an elf. In the story of Völund that is recounted in *Thidrek's Saga*, Egil is reputed to be an excellent archer.

EIKIN. One of the rivers that flow out of Hvergelmir.

EIKINSKJALDI. One of the dwarves in Dvalin's band, which left the rocks to settle on a sandy plain.

EIKTHYRNIR. The stag that stands in or on Valhalla and feeds on the branches of the tree called Laerad (presumably Yggdrasil). From its antlers, liquid drips down into Hvergelmir, enough to furnish water for all the streams that flow about the dwellings of the Aesir.

EINHERJAR. Odin's champions, the battle-slain warriors who come to Asgard. Each day they fight; each night—restored from their wounds—they feast in Valhalla, served by the valkyries.

EINRIDI. A nickname of Thor.

EIR. One of the Asynjur. She is the best physician.

EIR. One of the nine handmaidens of Menglod.

EISTLA. A giantess; one of the nine sisters who mothered Heimdall.

EITRI. A dwarf smith; the brother of Brokk. He created three gifts for the Aesir: Draupnir, Gullinbursti, and Mjöllnir, the latter being judged their most precious treasure—thus winning Brokk's wager with Loki. See also SINDRI.

ELDHRIMNIR. The kettle in Valhalla in which Andhrimnir nightly cooks the boar Saehrimnir to feed the Einherjar.

ELDIR. One of Aegir's servants. See also FIMAFENG.

ELIVAGAR. This name may apply to all the icy rivers that flow out of the spring Hvergelmir in Niflheim, but it appears to have been specifically used only in association with Fimbulthul, Fjörm, Gjöll, Gunnthro, Hrid, Leipt, Slid, Svol, Sylg, Vid, and Ylg.

ELJUDNIR. Hel's hall.

ELLI. The toothless old crone in Utgard who brought

Thor to his knees when they had a wrestling match. She is a personification of old age.

EMBLA. The first woman, who was created from a tree (presumably an elm) by Bor's sons.

ERNA. The wife of Jarl and mother of the class of noblefolk.

ETTIN. See JÖTUN.

EYRGJAFA. A giantess; one of the nine sisters who mothered Heimdall.

F

FADIR. The husband of Modir.

FAFNIR. A son of Hreidmar and brother of Oter, Regin, Lofnheid, and Lyngheid. He and Regin slew Hreidmar to obtain Oter's weregild. Fafnir refused to share the gold with Regin, taking it to Gnita Heath where he transformed himself into a dragon and settled down to guard his treasure. He was eventually slain by the hero Sigurd.

FAL. The name used for the dwarf Fjalar in the *Prose Edda*.

FALHOFNIR. A horse belonging to the Aesir.

FARBAUTI. The giant who fathered Loki by Laufey (or Nal).

FARMAGUD. A nickname of Odin.

FARMATYR. A nickname of Odin.

FENG. A nickname of Odin.

FENJA. One of the two giantesses bought by King Frodi to turn the magic mill Grotti. See also MENJA.

FENRIR. A giant wolf; a son of Loki and Angrboda, and brother of Hel and Jörmungand. After he grew large, the Aesir contrived to bind him (at the cost of Tyr's right hand) on the island Lyngvi where he shall remain until Ragnarök, at which time he will slay Odin. Fenrir, in turn, will be slain by Odin's son Vidar.

FENRIS-ULF. See FENRIR.

FENSALIR. Frigg's dwelling in Asgard.

FID. One of the dwarves in Dvalin's band, which left the rocks to settle on a sandy plain.

FILI. A dwarf.

FIMAFENG. A servant of Aegir who was slain out of spite by Loki. See also ELDIR.

FIMBULTHUL. One of the icy rivers in Niflheim that arise from the spring Hvergelmir. See also Elivagar.

FIMBULTYR. A nickname of Odin.

FIMBULVETR. A winter in which the snow will drive from all quarters, the frosts will be great, the winds biting, and the sun will give little warmth. Three such winters, with no intervening summers, shall precede Ragnarök. These winters themselves will be preceded by three other winters during which wars will be waged throughout the world, setting kinfolk against each other.

FINN. The name used for the dwarf Fid in Hollander's translation of the *Poetic Edda*.

FJALAR. One of the dwarves of Dvalin's band, which left the rocks to settle on a sandy plain. He and his brother, Galar, slew Kvasir and made a potent mead from his blood.

FJALAR. A nickname of the giant Suttung.

FJALAR. A nickname of the giant Skrymir.

FJALAR. The red cock whose crowing shall wake the giants for Ragnarök.

FJÖLKALD. Allegedly the grandfather of Vindkald, a fictitious name used by Svipdag in an attempt to deceive the giant Fjölsvid, who was guarding Menglod's abode.

FJÖLNIR. A legendary Swedish king at whose court King Frodi purchased the giantesses Fenja and Menja.

FJÖLNIR. A nickname of Odin.

FJÖLNIR'S PLEDGE. The eye that Odin (presumably using the name Fjölnir) had to exchange with Mimir for a drink from his sacred well.

FJÖLSVID. A nickname of Odin.

FJÖLSVID. The giant who guards Menglod's abode. He and Svipdag engaged in a lengthy question-and-answer exchange.

FJÖLVAR. Odin's companion during the five winters they spent fighting and wenching on the island Algrön.

FJÖRGVIN. See FJÖRGYN.

FJÖRGYN. A nickname of Jörd and, in its masculine form, Fjörgvin, of Odin.

FJÖRM. One of the icy rivers in Niflheim that arise from the spring Hvergelmir. See also ELIVAGAR.

FJÖRSVARTNIR. One of Nott's two horses. See also HRIMFAXI.

FOLKVANG. Freyja's homestead in Asgard.

FORNJOT. A giant; the father of Wind, Sea, and Fire.

FORSETI. The son of Balder and Nanna. He lives in Glitnir, where he sits in judgment on lawsuits—his is the best court known to gods and men.

FRAEG. A dwarf.

FRANANG. The waterfalls under which Loki—in salmon form—hid in fear of the Aesir after he had brought about the death of Balder.

FRAR. A dwarf.

FREKI. One of Odin's wolves, which he feeds from his table. See also GERI.

FREY. One of the Vanir; the son of Njörd, brother of Freyja, and husband of Gerd. Frey governs rainfall and sunshine, hence the fruitfulness of the earth. He is invoked by men for peace and prosperity. Fair of face and powerful, he will be slain by Surt at Ragnarök. The boar is his sacred animal.

FREYJA. One of the Vanir; the daughter of Njörd, sister of Frey, wife of Od, and mother of Hnoss and Gersimi. A beautiful and powerful goddess who drives a chariot drawn by two cats. On occasion, however, her steed is a golden-bristled boar, Hildisvini, fashioned by the dwarves Dain and Nabbi. Whenever she visits a battlefield she claims half of the slain. She enjoys love songs and is invoked for help in love affairs. The giants often

Odin and Freyja.

scheme to gain her in marriage for one of their number. She owns the Brisingamen necklace and a feather cloak that enables the wearer to assume the form of a falcon.

FREYJA'S TEARS. When Freyja's husband, Od, leaves her, she wanders the world seeking him. Her tears, shed because of his absence, become pieces of gold or amber.

FRID. One of the nine handmaidens of Menglod.

FRIGG. The wife of Odin and mother of Balder. She knows the fates of all men but offers no prophecies. Women invoke her aid at births.

FRODI. The son of Fridleif. A mighty, legendary Danish king, Frodi imposed his peace on the northern lands. He acquired the magic mill Grotti, which led to his demise.

FROSTI. One of the dwarves of Dvalin's band, which left the rocks to settle on a sandy plain.

FULLA. One of the Asynjur. She is a virgin who looks after Frigg's wardrobe and is her confidante.

FUNDIN. A dwarf.

FYLGJUR (singular, FYLGJA). Guardian spirits, one of which is associated with each person, that usually appear in the form of an animal (in a few instances they have been reported to look like a person of the opposite gender). A fylgja usually is visible only in a dream or to someone with "second sight."

G

GAGNRAD. A nickname used by Odin when he visited the giant Vafthrudnir.

GALAR. A dwarf; he and his brother, Fjalar, slew Kvasir and made a potent mead from his blood.

GANDALF. A dwarf, despite having an elvish name.

GANG. A giant; a son of Alvaldi and brother of Thjazi and Idi.

GANGLATI. Hel's manservant.

GANGLERI. The alias used by King Gylfi when he visited Asgard to learn about the powers of the Aesir.

GANGLERI. A nickname of Odin.

GANGLÖT. Hel's maidservant.

GARDROFA. A horse; the mother of Gna's stallion, Hofvarpnir.

GARM. The hound of Hel, which is chained at the mouth of Gnipa Cave. At Ragnarök he shall break loose to attack the Aesir, and he and Tyr will slay each other.

GASTROPNIR. The wall that encloses Menglod's dwelling. It was built from the giant Leirbrimir's limbs.

GAUT. A nickname of Odin.

GEFJON. One of the Asynjur. She is a virgin and all women who die virgins serve as her handmaidens. She has the gift of prophecy. Gefjon may be same person as Gefjun, but the latter is no virgin.

GEFJUN. A kinswoman of the Aesir. She had four sons by a giant in Jötunheim. When King Gylfi of Sweden promised her as much land as four oxen could plow up in a day and a night, she turned her sons into oxen and plowed so deep and wide a furrow that the land broke free from Sweden. The oxen pulled it into the western sea, and where they stopped Gefjun fixed the land and named it Selund, which is now the eastern part of Denmark.

GEFN. A nickname Freyja sometimes uses when she seeks her wandering husband, Od.

GEIRAHÖD. One of the valkyries.

GEIRONUL. One of the valkyries.

GEIRRÖD. A son of King Hraudung, who, at Odin's counsel, marooned his older brother, Agnar, and claimed the kingship vacated by their dead father. Acting upon a false warning from Frigg, who had fostered Agnar, Geirröd seized and tortured a disguised Odin, thinking him an evil wizard. Naturally this behavior alienated Odin, who then caused Geirröd to stumble and fall upon his own sword.

GEIRRÖD. A giant who forced Loki to trick Thor into visiting Geirröd's dwelling without his hammer, his belt of strength, or his iron gloves. Reequipped by the friendly giantess Grid, Thor thwarted Geirröd's scheme and slew him with a red-hot bar of iron that Thor threw through an iron pillar, Geirröd, and the wall of his house.

GEIRRÖDARGARD. Geirröd's dwelling in Jötunheim.

GEIRSKOGUL. One of the valkyries.

GEIRVIMUL. A river that flows out of Hvergelmir.

GELGJA. The chain to which the wolf Fenrir's fetter is fastened.

GERD. A giantess; the daughter of Gymir and Aurboda. She is the most beautiful of women and became the wife of Frey as a result of Skirnir's persuasiveness.

GERI. One of Odin's wolves, which he feeds from his table. See also FREKI.

GERI. One of the two great hounds that guard Menglod's hall. See also GIF.

GERSIMI. One of the daughters of Freyja and Od, or a nickname of their daughter Hnoss.

GESTUMBLINDI. A nickname of Odin.

GIF. One of the two great hounds that guard Menglod's hall. See also GERI.

GILLING. A giant who, with his wife, was murdered by the dwarves Fjalar and Galar. He was drowned and she had her head smashed with a millstone. Their sons were Baugi and Suttung.

GIMLE. Standing in the southern end of Vidblain, with its golden roof shining brighter than the sun, Gimle is the most beautiful hall in the heavens—and the only one that shall survive Ragnarök. Only Light Elves live there now, but after Ragnarök it shall become the dwelling place of good and righteous men.

GINNAR. One of the dwarves of Dvalin's band, which left the rocks to settle on a sandy plain.

GINNUNGAGAP. The Yawning Gap that preceded the formation of the Nine Worlds. Once Muspellheim and Niflheim were formed it lay between them. Where the heat of the former met the frost of the latter the frost melted and dripped, and from the venomous drops that formed grew Ymir—the first being.

GIPUL. One of the rivers that flow out of Hvergelmir.

GISL. A horse belonging to the Aesir.

GJALLARHORN. See GJÖLL.

GJALP. A giantess; a daughter of Geirröd. She first tried to drown Thor by causing the river Vimur to flood as he was crossing it; then she and her sister, Greip, tried to crush him against the rafters of Geirröd's dwelling. Thor resisted their push and broke their backs. A giantess with this name was one of the nine mothers of Heimdall.

GJÖLL. The horn from which Mimir drinks the water of wisdom, and which Heimdall will blow if the Hill Giants cross Bifröst.

GJÖLL. One of the icy rivers in Niflheim that arise from the spring Hvergelmir. It is the one that flows closest to Hel Gate. Its bridge is thatched with gold. See also ELIVAGAR.

GJÖLL. The boulder through which the chain Gelgja passes. Part of the anchorage for Fenrir's fetter.

GLAD. A horse belonging to Dag. See also SKINFAXI.

GLADSHEIM. The golden temple in Asgard that contains the high seat of Odin and the thrones of the Aesir.

GLAPSVID. A nickname of Odin.

GLASIR. A grove in Asgard that lies before the doors of Valhalla. Its foliage is pure gold.

GLEIPNIR. The fetter with which the great wolf Fenrir is bound. It was made by certain dwarves in Svartalfheim from the sound of a cat's footstep, a woman's beard, a mountain's roots, a bear's sinews, a fish's breath, and a bird's spittle. See also DROMI and LAEDING.

GLEN. A horse belonging to the Aesir.

GLEN. The husband of Sol.

GLER. A horse belonging to the Aesir.

GLITNIR. Forseti's dwelling in Asgard whose walls, posts, and pillars are made of red gold, and its roof of silver.

GLOIN. One of the dwarves of Dvalin's band, which left the rocks to settle on a sandy plain.

GNA. One of the Asynjur. She is Frigg's messenger, who travels everywhere on her horse, Hofvarpnir.

GNIPAHELLIR. The cave where the hound Garm is fettered, and shall remain so until Ragnarök. Presumably it is located along the road to Hel's domain.

GNITA HEATH. The place where Fafnir took his ill-gotten hoard and, in dragon form, guarded it until the hero Sigurd slew him.

GOIN. A serpent, a son of Grafvitnir, which lives in the spring Hvergelmir beneath the ash Yggdrasil and tears at its branches (rootlets?).

GÖLL. One of the valkyries.

GÖMUL. One of the rivers that flow out of Hvergelmir.

GÖNDLIR. A nickname of Odin.

GÖNDUL. One of the valkyries.

GÖPUL. One of the rivers that flow out of Hvergelmir.

GRABAK. One of the serpents that live in the spring Hvergelmir beneath the ash Yggdrasil and tear at its branches (rootlets?).

GRAD. One of the rivers that flow out of Hvergelmir.

GRAFVITNIR. The serpent that is father to Goin and Moin.

GRAFVÖLLUD. One of the serpents that live in the spring Hvergelmir beneath the ash Yggdrasil and tear at its branches (rootlets?).

GRAM. Sigurd's sword, reforged by Regin from the fragments of the sword Sigurd's father, Sigmund, had as a gift from Odin. It was so sharp that it sliced through a clump of wool that floated by it in a stream, and it also clove Regin's anvil to the ground.

GRANI. Sigurd's horse. A descendant of Sleipnir, it was given to Sigurd by Odin.

GREIP. A giantess; a daughter of Geirröd. She and her sister, Gjalp, tried to crush Thor against the roof of Geirröd's house. Thor pushed back and broke their backs. A giantess with this name was one of the nine mothers of Heimdall.

GRID. A giantess; the mother of Vidar the Silent by Odin. She enabled Thor to overcome the crafty giant Geirröd by loaning the god her belt of strength, iron gloves, and staff, as well as by warning about Geirröd's character.

GRID'S ROD. A powerful staff belonging to the giantess Grid, who lent it to Thor. It enabled him to ford the mighty Vimur and to defend himself against the attempts of the giantesses Gjalp and Greip to crush him in Geirröd's house.

GRIM. A nickname of Odin.

GRIMNIR. A nickname of Odin.

GRJOTUNAGARD. The place on the frontier between Asgard and Jötunheim where Thor and the giant Hrungnir fought their famous duel.

GROA. A wise woman; the wife of Aurvandil and mother of Svipdag (by Solbjart, her second husband). She sang spells over Thor to remove a fragment of Hrungnir's hone from the god's skull after the duel at Grjotunagard. The spell was not completed because Thor rewarded Groa before she had finished and she became so excited that she forgot the rest of the spell.

GROTTI. A magic mill that would grind out whatever was requested. It was turned by the giantesses Fenja and Menja. It was lost at sea while grinding salt, which is why seawater is salty.

GUD. One of the valkyries.

GULLFAXI. The giant Hrungnir's horse, which lost a race to Sleipnir. After the duel at Grjotunagard, Thor gave the horse to his son Magni.

GULLINBURSTI. The golden-bristled boar that draws Frey's chariot. It is also known as Slidrugtanni.

GULLINKAMBI. The cock whose crowing shall wake the gods and heroes in Asgard at Ragnarök.

GULLINTANNI. A nickname of Heimdall, which refers to his golden teeth.

GULLTOPP. The horse belonging to Heimdall.

GULLVEIG. Apparently a female Van who, for some reason, was first speared and then burned (unsuccessfully three times—each time she arose again like the Phoenix) by the Aesir in Odin's hall. Her mistreatment brought about the war between the Vanir and the Aesir. There is some indication she may have been a seeress and witch. See also HEID.

GUNGNIR. Odin's spear, which when hurled never missed its mark. It was made as a gift for him by the dwarves known as the sons of Ivaldi.

GUNN. One of the valkyries.

GUNNLÖD. A giantess; the daughter of Suttung. She guarded Kvasir's blood in Hnitbjörg, but Odin—in the guise of a giant—seduced her and stole the magic mead.

GUNNTHORIN. One of the rivers that flow out of the spring Hvergelmir in Niflheim. In the *Prose Edda* it is called Gunnthrain.

GUNNTHRO. One of the rivers that flow out of the spring Hvergelmir in Niflheim. See also ELIVAGAR.

GUST. Probably a nickname of the dwarf Andvari.

GYLFI. The Swedish king who gave Gefjun the grant of land which she (with the aid of her four sons in the guise of oxen) converted into the island of Selund. Gylfi visited Asgard and engaged in a dialogue with Odin, who appeared as three men seated on a three-tiered throne. That dialogue forms the bulk of "Gylfaginning," which supplies much of the mythological information presented in the *Prose Edda*.

GYLLIR. A horse belonging to the Aesir.

GYMIR. A nickname of Aegir.

GYMIR. A giant; the husband of the giantess Aurboda. Their daughter, Gerd, is the fairest of all women.

H

HABROK. It was said by the Aesir to be the foremost among hawks.

HAKI. A giant; a son of Hvedna.

HALLINSKIDI. A nickname of Heimdall, which refers to his association with the ram.

HAMSKERPIR. The sire of Gna's stallion, Hofvarpnir.

HANAR. A dwarf.

HANGAGUD. A nickname of Odin.

HAPTAGUD. A nickname of Odin.

HAR. A nickname of Odin, and the one he assumed while occupying the lowest seat of his three-tiered throne during the beguiling of King Gylfi. See also JAFNHAR and THRIDI.

HAR. A dwarf. There is some confusion in the various translations as to whether Har or Hör was a member of Dvalin's band, which left the rocks to settle on a sandy plain.

HARBARD. A nickname of Odin.

HATI HRODVITNISSON. Apparently an alternate name for Managarm.

HAUGSPORI. One of the dwarves in Dvalin's band, which left the rocks to settle on a sandy plain.

HEERFADIR. See HERJAFADIR.

HEFRING. One of the nine daughters of Aegir and Ran.

HEID. A giantess; perhaps the daughter of Hrimnir and sister of Hrossthjof.

HEID. A seeress and witch, she is the transformed Van Gullveig after she was burned three times by the Aesir, and each time restored.

HEIDDRAUPNIR. Apparently a nickname of Mimir.

HEIDRUN. The she-goat in Valhalla that stands in or atop the hall and bites off leaves from the famous tree Laerad (presumably Yggdrasil). From her udders flows the mead that is drunk by the Einherjar.

HEIMDALL. Often called the White God, Heimdall is the son of nine maidens—all sisters. He sits by the Asgard end of Bifröst to guard it from the Hill Giants. He rarely sleeps and has exceptionally keen senses of hearing and sight. He has a trumpet called Gjöll, which can be heard throughout the Nine Worlds, and he carries a sword called Hofud. At Ragnarök he and Loki, who contended before, shall slay each other. In the guise of Rig, Heimdall sired the three classes of

Norseman: thrall, freeman, and noble. Heimdall has teeth of gold, and the animal associated with him is the ram.

HEL. The daughter of Loki and Angrboda, and sister of Fenrir and Jörmungand. Exiled to Niflheim by Odin, she rules over those who die by accident or of old age. One-half of her body is blue-black, while the other half is flesh-colored; her countenance is grim and fierce.

HEL. Sometimes used to refer to Hel's realm as well as her person. It is a cold, damp place said to lie "northward and downward," apparently somewhere in Niflheim.

HELBLINDI. A giant; a son of Farbauti and Laufey, and brother of Loki and Byleist.

HELBLINDI. A nickname of Odin.

HEL GATE. The gate at the entrance to Hel's realm.

HELGRIND. The fence or wall surrounding Hel's realm.

HEL WAY. The road to Hel's realm.

HELM OF TERROR. A helmet belonging to Hreidmar, and taken by Fafnir, which was said to terrify all living creatures that see it.

HENGIKJÖPT. The man who gave the magic mill Grotti to King Frodi. Possibly a nickname of Odin.

HENGJANKJAPTA. A giantess wounded or killed by Thor.

HEPTIFILI. A dwarf.

Hermod and Sleipnir evade Garm, the hound of Hel.

HERFJÖTUR. One of the valkyries.

HERJAFADIR. A nickname of Odin.

HERJAN. A nickname of Odin.

HERMOD. A son of Odin, surnamed the Bold, who rode Sleipnir to Hel's realm seeking Balder's return.

HERSIR. The father of Erna.

HERTEIT. A nickname of Odin.

HERVOR. A valkyrie and swan-maiden; the daughter of Hlodver and sister of Hladgud. Hervor the Allwise became the wife of Völund, but after eight winters a compulsion to resume her role as a valkyrie caused her to fly off with her sister.

HILD. One of the valkyries.

HILDISVINI. Freyja's golden-bristled boar, fashioned for her by the dwarves Dain and Nabbi.

HILDOLF. Possibly a nickname of Odin. Hildolf was alleged to be a chieftain who lived by Rathsey Sound and assigned Odin (in the guise of Harbard) the task of ferrying travelers over the sound.

HIMINBJÖRG. Heimdall's dwelling in Asgard near the end of Bifröst.

HIMINBRJOT. The largest ox in the giant Hymir's herd. Thor used its head as bait when he went fishing for the Midgard Serpent.

HIMINGLAEVA. One of the nine daughters of Aegir and Ran.

HJALMBERI. A nickname of Odin.

HJORVARD. A giant; the father of Hvedna.

HJUKI. One of the two children (the other is his sister, Bil) who follow Mani through the heavens as he guides the course of the moon.

HLADGUD. A valkyrie and swanmaiden; the daughter

of Hlodver and sister of Hervor. Hladgud the Swanwhite became the wife of Slagfid, a brother of Völund, but after eight winters a compulsion to resume her role as a valkyrie caused her to fly off with her sister.

HLEBARD. A giant who gave his magic wand to Odin and was repaid by being rendered witless.

HLEDJOLF. The name applied to the dwarf Hlevang in the *Prose Edda.*

HLER. A nickname of Aegir.

HLESEY. Also known as Hles Isle and apparently identical with the Danish island of Laessö. An island associated with the sea god Aegir. There Thor encountered a band of female berserkers (battle-crazed warriors oblivious to pain) who carried iron clubs and attacked his ship.

HLEVANG. One of the dwarves of Dvalin's band, which left the rocks to settle on a sandy plain.

HLIDSKJALF. Odin's high seat whence he can look over the whole world and see what everyone is doing. The seat is situated in Asgard in the hall called Valaskjalf (which Hollander indicated is another name for Valhalla).

HLIF. One of the nine handmaidens of Menglod.

HLIFTHRASA. One of the nine handmaidens of Menglod.

HLIN. A nickname of Frigg.

HLIN. One of the Asynjur. She has been appointed to look after those men whom Frigg wishes to protect.

HLODVER. A king; the father of the swanmaidens Hervor and Hladgud.

HLOKK. One of the valkyries.

HLORA. A foster-daughter of Thor, according to Brodeur's translation (but Simek refers to her as Thor's foster-mother).

HLORRIDI. A nickname of Thor.

HLÖDYN. A nickname of Jörd.

HNIKAR. A nickname of Odin.

HNIKUD. A nickname of Odin.

HNITBJÖRG. The mountain where Suttung hid Kvasir's blood.

HNOSS. A daughter of Freyja and Od. She is so beautiful that everything lovely and precious bears her name. See also GERSIMI.

HODDMIMIR. According to Hollander, this is a nickname of the great ash tree Yggdrasil. It is said that two humans, Lif and Lifthrasir, will be sheltered in Hoddmimir's wood during Ragnarök and will give rise to the race of humans that will populate the New Earth. Other translators seem to think that Hoddmimir is a nickname of Mimir, and Hoddmimir's wood is a nickname of the tree.

HODDROFNIR. Apparently a nickname of Mimir.

HOENIR. One of the Aesir. Along with Mimir he was sent to the Vanir as a hostage. According to the *Poetic Edda,* it was he who gave Ask and Embla awareness. He will serve as priest of those Aesir who will reoccupy Asgard following Ragnarök.

HOFUD. Heimdall's sword.

HOFVARPNIR. Gna's horse; his sire was Hamskerpir, his dam Gardrofa. Hofvarpnir runs through the air and over the sea.

HORN. See HRÖN.

HORNBORI. A dwarf.

HÖD. One of the Aesir; a son of Odin. The blind, but extremely strong, god who was tricked by Loki into killing his brother Balder with a mistletoe dart. Höd, in turn, was slain by Vali. Höd, with Balder, is fated to return to Asgard when the world is reborn after Ragnarök.

HÖLL. One of the rivers that flow out of Hvergelmir.

HÖR. See HAR (a dwarf).

HÖRN. A nickname Freyja sometimes use when she seeks her wandering husband, Od.

HRAESVELG. A giant who, in the form of an eagle, sits at the northern end of heaven (presumably atop Yggdrasil). When he spreads his wings the wind arises from beneath them.

HRAUDING. The king who was father of Agnar and Geirröd.

HREIDMAR. The father of Lofnheid, Lyngheid, Oter, Fafnir, and Regin. The latter two slew him to obtain Oter's weregild. Hreidmar was a wealthy farmer who was well versed in black magic.

HRID. One of the icy rivers in Niflheim that arise from the spring Hvergelmir. See also ELIVAGAR.

HRIMFAXI. The horse that draws Nott's chariot through the heavens. The foam from his bit forms the morning dew. See also FJÖRSVARTNIR.

HRIMGRIMNIR. A giant in Niflheim, marriage to whom Skirnir threatened Gerd if she would not agree to wed Frey.

HRIMNIR. A Frost Giant; a kinsman (perhaps father) of Heid and Hrossthjof.

HRINGHORNI. Balder's ship on which his funeral pyre was lighted.

HRIST. One of the valkyries.

HROD. A giant.

HRODVITNIR. A nickname of Fenrir.

HROPT. A nickname of Odin.

HROPTATYR. A nickname of Odin.

HROSSTHJOF. A giant; perhaps the son of Hrimnir and brother of Heid.

HROTTI. Fafnir's sword. It was taken by the hero Sigurd after he slew Fafnir.

HRÖN. One of the rivers that flow out of Hvergelmir.

HRÖN. One of the nine daughters of Aegir and Ran.

HRUNGNIR. A giant who lived in Jötunheim. After losing a horse race to Odin, he rode into Asgard where he got into a fracas with Thor. In the subsequent duel at Grjotunagard, he was slain by Thor's hammer. Hrungnir's heart, head, and shield were all of stone, and his weapon was a hone. Thjalfi tricked the giant into standing on his shield so it could not be used as protection against Mjöllnir.

HRUNGNIR'S HEART. A written character (a rune?) shaped like the heart of that giant, which was stone and pointed with three corners.

HRYM. The giant who shall steer the ship Naglfar to meet the Aesir at Ragnarök (another version says this will be Loki's role). The ship will carry the hosts of Muspellheim.

HUGI. The young Utgard giant who beat Thjalfi in a foot race. He is a personification of Utgard-Loki's thought.

HUGIN. One of the two ravens that sit on Odin's shoulders and tell him all that they see and hear during their wanderings through the world. See also MUNIN.

HUGSTARI. The name used by the dwarf Haugspori in the *Prose Edda*.

HVEDNA. A giantess; the daughter of Hjorvard and mother of Haki.

HVEDRUNG. Probably a nickname of Loki.

HVERGELMIR. The great spring that wells up in the center of Niflheim and is the source of numerous rivers. See ELIVAGAR.

HYMIR. A giant; the father of Tyr. Hymir inadvertently accompanied Thor on his fishing expedition for the Midgard Serpent. Hymir was later slain by Thor when he tried to prevent the god from carrying off the enormous cauldron Thor had won from him.

HYNDLA. A wise giantess who lives in a cave and rides a wolf. She was forced by Freyja to tell her heroic protege Ottar the lore he needed to know to win a wager with another hero, Angantyr.

HYRROKKIN. The giantess whom the Aesir called upon to launch Balder's funeral ship. She rode a wolf and had a pair of vipers for reins.

I

IDAVOLL. The plain near the center of Asgard where Gladsheim and Vingolf are situated. It is the meeting place of the Aesir.

IDI. A giant; the son of Alvaldi and brother of Thjazi and Gang. Presumably he is an uncle of Fenja, Menja, or both.

IDUN. The wife of Bragi. She provides the Aesir with the apples of youth, which she keeps in an ashwood box.

IFING. An ice-free river that flows between Asgard and Utgard.

IM. A giant; the son of Vafthrudnir.

IMD. A giantess; one of the nine mothers of Heimdall.

INGUN. The sister of Njörd and mother by him of Frey and Freyja.

IRI. One of the nine dwarves who constructed the hall called Lyr, where Menglod dwelled.

IRON WOOD. See JARNVID.

IVALDI. A dwarf; the father of the unnamed dwarves who crafted the ship Skidbladnir, the spear Gungnir, and Sif's golden hair.

J

JAFNHAR. A nickname of Odin, and the one he assumed in occupying the middle seat of his three-tiered throne during the beguiling of King Gylfi. See also HAR and THRIDI.

JALK. A nickname of Odin.

JARI. A dwarf.

JARL. The son of Rig and Modir; the progenitor of Norse noblemen.

JARNSAXA. The giantess by whom Thor fathered Magni (and perhaps Modi). A giantess with this name was one of the nine mothers of Heimdall.

JARNVID. The Iron Wood, which lies to the east of Midgard, is the home of an ancient giantess and her brood (all of whom are in the form of wolves) as well as a bevy of troll women, the Jarnvidjur.

JARNVIDJUR. The troll women who dwell in the Iron Wood.

JOR. A horse that belongs to the Aesir.

JÖRD. A giantess; the daughter of Nott and Annar, wife of Odin, and mother of Thor.

JÖRMUNGAND. The Midgard Serpent; a son of Loki and Angrboda, and brother of Fenrir and Hel. Thrown into the ocean by the Aesir, he has grown so huge that he encircles the world and grasps his own tail in his mouth. He and Thor are each other's nemesis.

JÖRUVELLIR. The site of Aurvangar to which the dwarves from Svarinshaug came.

JÖTUN. A member of one of the races of giants: the Hill Giants, Frost Giants, and Fire Giants. They seem to vary considerably in size, appearance, and disposition.

Loki's Children: Hel, ruler of the Dead; Jörmungand, the Midgard Serpent; and Fenrir, a giant wolf.

A number of them possess great wisdom and magical skills, including shape changing. Some of the females are notable for their beauty. Despite the enmity that exists between them, the Aesir are descendants of the giants.

JÖTUNHEIM. The land of the giants, which lies somewhere to the east of Midgard.

K

KARL. The son of Rig and Amma; the progenitor of Norse freemen.

KEILA. A giantess whose head Thor smote.

KERLAUGAR. Two of the four streams Thor must wade each day when he goes to the court at Urd's Well. Their individual names are not given. See also KÖRMT and ÖRMT.

KILI. A dwarf.

KJALAR. A nickname of Odin.

KJALLANDI. A giantess whom Thor smashed altogether.

KJAR. The king of Valland and father of the valkyrie Olrun.

KOLGA. One of the nine daughters of Aegir and Ran.

KOR. Hel's bed.

KÖRMT. One of the four streams Thor must wade each day when he goes to the court by Urd's Well. See also KERLAUGAR and ÖRMT.

KVASIR. Formed from the spittle of the Aesir and Vanir, he allegedly was the wisest among them. It was Kvasir who perceived that Loki had invented the fish net (to anticipate ways in which he, in salmon form, might be trapped) and reconstructed one from ashes in the fire-place where Loki had burned it. Kvasir was killed by two dwarves, who took his blood and mixed it with honey to make a potent mead.

KVASIR'S BLOOD. The mead made from the blood of Kvasir by his murderers, the dwarves Kjalar and Galar. Those who drink from it will become skalds or scholars.

L

LAEDING. The first fetter placed on the great wolf Fenrir and one that he easily broke. See also DROMI and GLEIPNIR.

LAEGJARN. A nickname of Loki.

LAERAD. The famous tree in Valhalla on whose leaves the goat Heidrun feeds. This is probably a nickname of Yggdrasil.

LAEVATEIN. A rune-sword forged by Loki beneath Niflheim. It was kept by Sinmara in an iron chest bound by nine locks. Only with this weapon could the cock Vidofnir be slain.

LAUFEY. Probably a giantess; the mother of Loki by the giant Farbauti.

LEIDI. A giant slain by Thor.

LEIKN. A giantess whose leg was broken by Thor.

LEIPT. One of the icy rivers that arise from the spring Hvergelmir in Niflheim. See also ELIVAGAR.

LEIRBRIMIR. A giant from whose limbs Fjölsvid built the wall called Gastropnir.

LETTFETI. A horse belonging to the Aesir.

LIF. One of the two humans who will survive Ragnarök and become a progenitor of the new human race. They will be protected in Hoddmimir's wood, where they shall feed on the morning dew.

LIFTHRASIR. One of the two humans who will survive Ragnarök sheltered in Hoddmimir's wood.

LIGHT ELVES. See ALFAR.

LISTI. Probably a giant.

LIT. The dwarf who ran in front of Thor while he was consecrating Balder's funeral pyre and was unceremoniously kicked onto the pyre and consumed in the flames.

LJOSALFAR. The Light Elves.

LODDFAFNIR. A sage or bard to whom Odin gave a great deal of advice. A portion of the "Havamal" in the *Poetic Edda* is addressed to him.

LODUR. The god who, according to the *Poetic Edda*, gave Ask and Embla warmth and brought the color of life to their skins. Bellows has suggested that Lodur is a nickname of Loki.

LOFAR. A descendant of Dvalin's band of dwarves.

LOFN. One of the Asynjur. It is she who obtains permission from either Odin or Frigg for men and women to marry.

LOFNHEID. A daughter of Hreidmar and sister of Lyngheid, Oter, Fafnir, and Regin.

LOGI. The Utgard giant who defeated Loki in their famous eating contest by consuming not only the meat, but the bones and wooden trough as well. He is a personification of uncontrolled fire.

LOKI. A son of the giant Farbauti and Laufey (or Nal), and brother of Byleist and Helblindi. He is handsome but has a fickle and evil disposition. He surpasses all others in cunning. He would continually get the Aesir into predicaments, then extricate them with his craftiness. By Sigyn he fathered Nari and Vali; by Angrboda he fathered Fenrir, Jörmungand, and Hel. On one occasion he reversed roles and mothered Sleipnir. His role in the death of Balder led the Aesir to bind Loki to three stones and to fasten a serpent above him to drip venom on his face. There he shall remain until Ragnarök when he and Heimdall will slay each other.

LONI. A dwarf.

LOPT. A nickname of Loki.

LUTR. A giant slain by Thor.

LYFJABERG. The "spearpoint"-topped mountain on which Lyr, Menglod's hall, is balanced.

LYNGHEID. A daughter of Hreidmar and sister of Lofnheid, Oter, Fafnir, and Regin.

LYNGVI. The island in the lake Amsvartnir where the great wolf Fenrir is bound.

LYR. The hall in which Menglod resides. Simek suggested that the correct name is Hyr.

M

MAGNI. A son of Thor and the giantess Jarnsaxa, and brother of Modi and Thrud. Only Magni, when but three nights old, was able to lift the dead giant Hrungnir's foot off the fallen Thor after the conclusion of the famous duel at Grjotunagard. He will be one of those Aesir who shall survive Ragnarök.

MANAGARM. The most formidable of the race of troll-wolves fathered by Fenrir and mothered by the Hag of the Iron Wood. It is he that at Ragnarök shall feed on the flesh of the dead and swallow the moon. Simek, on the other hand, said that Managarm is another name for Fenrir.

MANI. The son of Mundilfari and brother of Sol. He was set in the heavens by the Aesir to guide the course of the moon and to determine its waxing and waning. He took along two children, Bil and Hjuki, who always follow him.

MANNHEIM. See MIDGARD.

MARDÖLL. A nickname Freyja sometimes uses when she seeks her wandering husband, Od.

MEGINGJARDIR. Thor's belt of strength. When he wears it, his strength is increased by half—or doubled (the translations vary).

MEILI. A brother of Thor.

MENGLOD. The beautiful woman who lived in an enchanted castle guarded by a giant, and who could only be won by the hero Svipdag.

MENJA. One of the two giantesses bought by King Frodi to turn the magic mill Grotti.

MIDGARD. Strictly speaking, the protective ramparts around the middle part of the earth formed from Ymir's eyebrows. The name has been more widely applied to the entire area so enclosed, and in which humans dwell. In the latter context it may be the equivalent of the rarely used Mannheim.

MIDGARD SERPENT. See JÖRMUNGAND.

MIDVITNIR A giant; the father of Sokkmimir.

MIMAMEID. A nickname of the ash tree Yggdrasil.

MIMIR. A giant; the son of Bölthorn and brother of Bestla (Odin's mother). He was the keeper of the well of wisdom (Mimir's Well) that lies beneath Yggdrasil's root in Jötunheim. The well was the source of Mimir's

Odin sacrifices an eye for a drink from Mimir's Well.

wisdom, since he drank its waters each day from the horn Gjöll (the *Voluspa* says he drank from Odin's eye). Mimir, along with Hoenir, was sent as a hostage to the Vanir who, disgusted with Hönir's inability to say anything for himself, cut off Mimir's head and sent it back to Odin. He preserved the head and consults it for hidden wisdom.

MIMIR'S WELL. The well or, more likely, spring that lies in Jötunheim beneath one root of Yggdrasil, in which wisdom and understanding are hidden.

MIST. One of the valkyries.

MISTARBLINDI. A giant; the father of Aegir.

MJÖDVITNIR. A dwarf.

MJÖLLNIR. Thor's hammer, which he has used to crack the skull of many a giant. On one occasion the giant Thrym stole the hammer. The hammer is a bit short in the handle due to Loki's efforts to distract the dwarves who forged it. Nevertheless, it has the remarkable trait of returning by itself to Thor's hand whenever he throws it.

MODGUD. The maiden who guards the bridge over the river Gjöll on Hel Way.

MODI. A son of Thor and brother of Magni and Thrud; although it often is assumed that his mother is Jarnsaxa, this fact is not explicitly stated in the *Eddas*. With his brother, Modi is destined to survive Ragnarök.

MODIR. The wife of Fadir and mother of Jarl (by Rig).

MOGTHRASIR. A collective, symbolic term for humankind.

MOIN. A serpent, a son of Grafvitnir, which lives in the spring Hvergelmir beneath the ash Yggdrasil and tears at its branches (rootlets?).

MOTSOGNIR. The mightiest ruler of the dwarves.

MÖKKURKALFI. The clay giant made to be a helper to Hrungnir when he fought Thor at Grjotunagard. He was nine miles tall and three miles broad at the armpits, and he was given a mare's heart. Despite his great size, he was so terrified when Thor appeared that he wet himself. After Thor slew Hrungnir, Thjalfi easily dispatched Mökkurkalfi.

MUNDILFARI. The man who was father to Mani and Sol.

MUNIN. One of the two ravens that sit on Odin's shoulders and tell him all they see and hear during their wanderings through the world. See also HUGIN.

MUSPELLHEIM. The oldest of the Nine Worlds. It lies in the southern region and is a land of fire that cannot be tolerated by anyone who is not a native thereof. Surt, a Fire Giant, guards Muspellheim with a flaming sword.

MYRKVID. A dark, magical forest that lies between Muspellheim and the more northern reaches of the world.

MYSING. The sea king who slew King Frodi and took the magic mill Grotti, which soon led to his doom, too.

N

NABBI. One of the two dwarf smiths who fashioned Freyja's golden-bristled boar, Hildisvini. See also DAIN.

NAGLFAR. The largest of all ships. It is made of dead men's nails and will carry the host of Muspellheim to Ragnarök. The giant Hrym will be its steersman (one version assigns this role to Loki).

NAGLFARI. The first husband of the giantess Nott and father of Aud.

NAGRIND. The gate or entrance into Hel's realm, i.e., Hel Gate.

NAIN. A dwarf.

NAL. See LAUFEY.

NALI. A dwarf.

NANNA. One of the Asynjur; the daughter of Nep, wife of Balder, and mother of Forseti. Following Balder's death, she died of a broken heart and traveled to Hel's realm on the same burning ship as he.

NAR. A dwarf.

NARFI. See NARI.

NARI. A son of Sigyn and Loki. The Aesir caused his brother Vali to turn into a wolf and tear him apart. Then they took Nari's intestines and bound his father, Loki, to three boulders.

NASTRAND. The place in Niflheim whereupon stands the hall-of-serpents to which murderers and oath breakers will go after Ragnarok to wade the rivers of venom spewed forth by the serpents. Its doors face northward.

NEP. The father of Nanna.

NIDAFJÖLL. See NIDAVELLIR.

Nidhögg and friends in Hvergelmir.

NIDAVELLIR. The dark mountains on which stands the dwarves' hall called Sindri.

NIDHÖGG. The dragon that gnaws on the root of Yggdrasil that lies in Niflheim. He lives in the spring Hvergelmir with a multitude of serpents and feeds on human corpses.

NIDI. A dwarf.

NIDUD. The king of the Njarar who had Völund hamstrung so the smith would be forced to labor for him.

NIFLHEIM. The ninth, and lowest, world. The realm of Hel and the abode of the dead are located here.

NIKAR. A nickname of Odin.

NIKUD. A nickname of Odin.

NINE DAUGHTERS of AEGIR and RAN. Blodughadda, Bylgja, Dröfn, Dufa, Hefring, Himinglaeva, Hrön, Kolga, and Ud (or Unn). They are personifications of ocean waves.

NINE DWARVES WHO BUILT MENGLOD'S HALL. Bari, Delling, Dori, Iri, Ori, Uni, Uri, Var, and Vegdrasil.

NINE HANDMAIDENS of MENGLOD. Aurboda, Bjort, Bleik, Blid, Eir, Frid, Hlif, Hlifthrasa, and Thjodvara.

NINE MOTHERS of HEIMDALL. The giant maidens, all sisters, who gave birth to Heimdall: Angeya, Atla, Eistla, Eyrgjafa, Gjalp, Greip, Imd, Jarnsaxa, and Ulfrun. Some mythographers consider Heimdall's mothers to be personifications of ocean waves so, despite the differences in names, they may be the nine daughters of Aegir and Ran.

NINE WORLDS. Asgard, Vanaheim, Alfheim, Midgard (=Mannheim?), Jötunheim, Muspellheim, Svartalfheim, and Niflheim. The identity of the ninth world is in doubt; several writers have suggested it should be Nidavellir, but this solution carries with it the problem of implying that the dwarves and Dark Elves are different races. The ninth world may be Hel's realm, but that is usually considered to be a part of Niflheim.

NIPING. A dwarf.

NJÖRD. A Van; the father of Frey and Freyja by his sister, Ingun. He rules the winds and calms the sea and fire; he is invoked by seafarers and fishermen. He is so wealthy that he can bestow land or possessions on those men who ask for them. He and his children came to the Aesir as hostages. The giantess Skadi was tricked into marrying him as part of her father Thjazi's weregild. It proved to be a mutually unsatisfactory marriage since she loved the mountains and he the sea.

NOATUN. The abode of Njörd that lies both in Asgard and near the sea.

NORDRI. A dwarf; one of the four who hold up Ymir's skull (i.e., the sky). See also AUSTRI, SUDRI, and VESTRI.

NORI. A dwarf.

NORNS. Certain women—some of Aesir-kin, some elves, some dwarves—one of whom comes to each new-born child and determines the nature of its life. Norns reflect their own ancestry and those from good stock apportion good lives; evil norns, on the other hand, decree misfortune for their charges. The chief Norns are Urd, Verdandi, and Skuld. Each morning they apply a watery mixture of clay from Urd's Well to Yggdrasil so its limbs will not wither or decay.

NOTT. The dark, swarthy daughter of the giant Nörfi. By her first husband, Naglfari, she had a son, Aud. By her second husband, Annar, she had a daughter, Jörd. By her third husband, Delling (one of the Aesir), she had a son, Dag. Nott and Dag were each given a chariot by Odin and set in the heavens to ride around the world each day, the mother leading. Nott is a personification of night.

NÖN. One of the rivers that flow out of Hvergelmir.

NÖRFI. The Jötunheim giant who was the father of Nott.

NÖT. One of the rivers that flow out of Hvergelmir.

NYI. A dwarf.

NYR. A dwarf.

NYRAD. A dwarf.

NYT. One of the rivers that flow out of Hvergelmir.

O

OD. The husband of Freyja and father of Hnoss and Gersimi. He often goes away on long journeys, which causes Freyja to weep golden tears. Some have suggested that this is a nickname of Odin.

ODIN. A son of Bor and Bestla, and brother of Vili and Ve. He is the highest and eldest of the Aesir, who obey him as children obey their father—which, for most of them, he is. He is a master shape changer, but often journeys in the guise of an old one-eyed man wearing a dark blue cloak.

ODRÖRIR. The kettle used by Fjalar and Galar to collect Kvasir's blood. See also BODN and SON.

OFNIR. One of the serpents that live in the spring Hvergelmir beneath the ash Yggdrasil and tear at its branches (rootlets?).

OFNIR. A nickname of Odin.

OIN. A dwarf, the father of Andvari, both of whom were members of Dvalin's band, which left the rocks to settle on a sandy plain.

OKOLNIR. That region in which stands the giant Brimir's beer hall.

OLRUN. A valkyrie and swanmaiden; the daughter of King Kjar. Olrun the Wise married Völund's brother Egil, but after eight winters a compulsion to resume her role as a valkyrie caused her to fly off.

OMI. A nickname of Odin.

ONAR. A dwarf.

ONAR. See ANNAR.

ORI. One of the nine dwarves who constructed the hall called Lyr where Menglod dwelled. A dwarf by this name was one of Dvalin's band, which left the rocks to settle on a sandy plain.

OSKI. A nickname of Odin.

OSKOPNIR. The place where the Aesir and Surt will meet in combat at Ragnarök. It may be the same as Vigrid.

OTER. A son of Hreidmar and brother of Fafnir, Regin, Lofnheid, and Lyngheid. A shape changer who was slain by Loki while in otter form. Loki stole sufficient weregild from the dwarf Andvari to fill and cover the otter skin.

OTTAR. Freyja's protege, a hero whom she helped to win a genealogical contest with another hero, Angantyr, by tricking the wise giantess Hyndla into disclosing this lore to Freyja while Ottar was present in the guise of a boar.

ÖRMT. One of the four streams Thor must wade each day when he goes to the court by Urd's Well. See also KERLAUGAR and KÖRMT.

R

RADGRID. One of the valkyries.

RADSEY. A sound near which the chieftain Hildof dwelled.

RADSVID. A dwarf.

RAGNARÖK. The great and final conflict between the gods and giants and their respective allies. It will be preceded by Fimbulvetr and will result in the destruction of most of the Nine Worlds.

RAN. The wife of Aegir. She rules over those who drown in the sea.

RANDGRID. One of the valkyries.

RATATÖSK. The squirrel that scampers up and down the ash Yggdrasil bearing insults between the eagle (presumably Hraesvelg) that sits atop the tree and the dragon Nidhögg, which lives beneath it.

RATI. The auger used by Odin (as Bölverk) to bore through rock to the cave in Hnitbjörg where Gunnlöd guarded Kvasir's blood.

REFIL. Regin's sword.

REGIN. A son of Hreidmar and brother of Oter, Fafnir, Lofnheid, and Lyngheid. After conspiring with Fafnir to slay their father for Oter's weregild, Regin was driven off by the treacherous Fafnir. Nursing his grievance against his brother, Regin enticed his fosterling, Sigurd, to become his instrument of vengeance. When Regin's intention to slay Sigurd (rather than share the treasure) was revealed by some birds, Sigurd killed Regin, too. Regin was said to be a dwarf in stature, though presumably he was not of that race; perhaps his having the same name as the dwarf Regin led to a confusion of their identities.

REGIN. A dwarf.

REGINLEIF. One of the valkyries.

REKK. The name used for the dwarf Regin in the *Prose Edda.*

RIG. The nickname used by Heimdall when he traveled through Midgard fathering the three classes of Norsemen: thralls, freemen, and nobles.

RIN. One of the rivers that flow out of Hvergelmir.

RIND. The mother of Vali by Odin. She is either one of the Asynjur or a giantess.

RINNANDI. One of the rivers that flow out of Hvergelmir.

RITHIL. See REFIL.

ROTA. One of the valkyries.

RÖSKVA. The daughter of Egil, sister of Thjalfi, and servant of Thor. She accompanied Thor, Loki, and her brother on their visit to the wily giant Utgard-Loki.

RUD. A river. See UD.

S

SAD. A nickname of Odin.

SAEG. The cask or bucket in which Bil and Hjuki carried water from the well Byrgir.

SAEHRIMNIR. The boar that provides meat for Valhalla. He is boiled every day and is whole again each evening.

SAEVERSTAD. The island on which King Nidud confined the hamstrung Völund.

SAGA. One of the Asynjur, and possibly a nickname of Frigg. Each day she and Odin drink from golden cups in her hall, Sökkvabekk.

SALGOLFNIR. A nickname of the cock Gullinkambi.

SAMSEY. The island on which Loki alleged that Odin wove spells like a witch.

SANNGETAL. A nickname of Odin.

SEKIN. A river that flows out of Hvergelmir.

SESSRUMNIR. Freyja's hall, which is large and beautiful.

SID. A river that flows out of Hvergelmir.

SIDGRANI. A nickname of Odin.

SIDHÖTT. A nickname of Odin.

SIDSKEGG. A nickname of Odin.

SIF. The wife of Thor and mother of Ull (by her first husband) and Thrud. According to Branston (1955, *Gods of the North*), Sif's first husband was Aurvandil. Her beautiful golden hair once was cut off by Loki but was replaced by hair of living gold that was magically produced by the dwarves.

SIGFÖD. A nickname of Odin.

SIGTYR. A nickname of Odin.

SIGURD. The son of Sigmund. He slew the dragon Fafnir (for which deed he was later known as Sigurd Fafnirsbane) and Fafnir's brother Regin. He acquired Fafnir's hoard and with it the ring that bore Andvari's curse. The subsequent working out of the curse lies in the realm of the semihistorical, and interested readers are urged to follow it in the *Volsunga Saga*.

SIGYN. The wife of Loki and mother of Nari and Vali. After Loki was bound by the Aesir, she remained beside him with a basin to catch the venom that dripped onto his face from a poisonous snake that Skadi had fastened above his head.

SILFRINTOPP. A horse belonging to the Aesir.

SIMUL. The pole on which the bucket Saeg was suspended.

SINDRI. A hall made of red gold that stands on Nidavellir. A dwelling of the dwarves, it is one of those halls in which good men shall reside after Ragnarök.

SINDRI. The name used for the dwarf Eitri in Brodeur's translation of the *Prose Edda*.

SINGASTEIN. The place where Heimdall and Loki, in the form of seals, contended for possession of the Brisingamen.

SINIR. A horse belonging to the Aesir.

SINMARA. The wife of Surt. She is custodian of the rune-sword Laevatein.

SJÖFN. One of the Asynjur. She turns the thoughts of men and women to love, and it is from her name that the Old Norse word for love (sjafni) comes.

SKADI. A giantess; the daughter of Thjazi. She married Njörd, but they separated because she couldn't bear to live by the sea, and he loathed the mountains where her home, Thrymheim, lies. There she dwells and hunts wild animals with her bow and arrows. She is sometimes called the Snowshoe Goddess (probably referring to a short ski used in wooded areas; there is no archaeological evidence that the true snowshoe was used in Scandinavia as early as Viking times).

SKAFID. One of the dwarves in Dvalin's band, which left the rocks to settle on a sandy plain.

SKEGGJÖLD. One of the valkyries.

SKEIDBRIMIR. A horse belonging to the Aesir.

SKIDBLADNIR. The foremost of ships, it was made for Frey by the sons of the dwarf Ivaldi. It is large enough to hold all of the Aesir and their weapons, but when not in use it can be folded up and kept in a pouch. Whenever its sails are hoisted a favorable wind blows up.

SKILFING. A nickname of Odin.

SKINFAXI. The horse that draws Dag's chariot through the heavens. The light from his mane illumines the whole earth and sky. See also GLAD.

SKIRNIR. Frey's messenger. He sought Gerd's hand for Frey and was rewarded with Frey's sword.

SKIRVIR. One of the dwarves in Dvalin's band, which left the rocks to settle on a sandy plain.

Skadi, a giantess, hunts wild animals with her bow and arrows.

SKOLL. The wolf that pursues the sun and will, at Ragnarök, capture her. A son of the Iron Wood hag and Fenrir.

SKÖGUL. One of the valkyries.

SKRYMIR. The nickname used by the giant Utgard-Loki when he deceived Thor and his companions on their journey to Utgard.

SKULD. One of the three Norns who live in a beautiful hall near Urd's Well. They determine the duration of each man's life. Skuld is the youngest Norn, and according to the *Prose Edda* always rides out (in company with the valkyries Gud and Rota) to decide the outcome of battles and choose the slain. In the *Poetic Edda,* there is a valkyrie who bears this name, too. See also URD and VERDANDI.

SKULD. One of the valkyries.

SLAGFID. The brother of Völund and Egil, and husband of the valkyrie Hladgud. They lived in Ulfdalir. When, in the ninth year, she and her sister valkyries flew off through Myrkvid to the wars, Slagfid fared southward to hunt for her. Since Völund is addressed as "elflord" by Nidud, presumably Slagfid is also an elf.

SLEIPNIR. Odin's gray, eight-legged horse. He is the offspring of the stallion Svadilfari and Loki (in mare's form). Sleipnir can travel over water and through the air as easily as over land.

SLID. One of the icy rivers in Niflheim that arise from the spring Hvergelmir. See also ELIVAGAR.

SLIDRUGTANNI. The boar that draws Frey's chariot. It is also known as Gullinbursti.

SNOTRA. One of the Asynjur. She is so wise and gentle that any person who possesses these attributes is said to be *snotr*.

SNÖR. The wife of Karl and mother of the class of freemen.

SOKKMIMIR. A giant, the son of Midvitnir, who was slain by Odin.

SOL. The daughter of Mundilfari and sister of Mani. The Aesir, angered by Mundilfari's presumption in thinking his children were as beautiful as the sun and moon, forced Sol to drive the chariot of the sun and Mani to guide the course of the moon. She is considered to be one of the Asynjur.

SOLBJART. The second husband of the wise-woman Groa and father of Svipdag.

SOLBLINDI. An ancestral dwarf, i.e., the dwarves are sometimes referred to as the "sons of Solblindi." Since the name means "sunblinded" and the dwarves call the sun "Dvalin's Doom," it seems possible that Solblindi is a nickname of Dvalin.

SON. One of the two vats used by Fjalar and Galar to collect Kvasir's blood. See also BODN and ODRÖRIR.

SÖKKVABEKK. Saga's large abode in Asgard.

STARKAD. A giant injured or slain by Thor.

STROND. A river that flows through Midgard and thence into Hel's domain.

SUDRI. A dwarf; one of the four who hold up Ymir's skull (i.e., the sky). See also AUSTRI, NORDRI, and VESTRI.

SUMAR. A giant; the son of Svasud.

SURT. A Fire Giant; the husband of Sinmara. The powerful ruler of the Sons of Muspell, who will lead them against the Aesir at Ragnarök and slay Frey with his fiery sword. Thereafter he shall destroy the whole world with his sword's flames.

SUTTUNG. A giant; a son of Gilling, brother of Baugi, and father of Gunnlöd. He obtained the mead made from Kvasir's blood as weregild (compensation) for the murder of his parents by the dwarves Fjalar and Galar. Giants, generally, are sometimes referred to as the "sons of Suttung."

SUTTUNG'S MEAD. See KVASIR'S BLOOD.

SVADILFARI. The stallion that helped its giant master haul the rocks to build the wall around Asgard. He fathered Sleipnir by Loki (in mare's form).

SVAFNIR. One of the serpents that live in the spring Hvergelmir beneath the ash Yggdrasil and tear at its branches (rootlets?).

SVAFNIR. A nickname of Odin.

SVAFRTHORIN. Menglod's paternal grandfather.

Surt, a Fire Giant, the husband of Sinmara.

SVALIN. The shield that is held before the sun.

SVARANG. A giant. In "The Lay of Harbard," the giants collectively are referred to as the "sons of Svarang."

SVARINSHAUG. The place of origin of the dwarves who went from there to Aurvangar on Jöruplain. Presumably the migration of Dvalin's band is involved.

SVARTALFAR (singular, SVARTALF). According to all sources, the Dark Elves are the same as the dwarves. They were described as having faces blacker than pitch. The similarity in name to the Light Elves is puzzling for it appears to be the only thing the two folk have in common.

SVARTALFHEIM. The world of the Dark Elves.

SVARTHÖFDI. The progenitor of all sorcerers.

SVASUD. The father of Sumar, who is of such a pleasant disposition that whatever is pleasant is called after him.

SVIAR. A dwarf.

SVIDRIR. A nickname of Odin.

SVIDUR. A nickname of Odin.

SVIPAL. A nickname of Odin.

SVIPDAG. The son of the wise-woman Groa and Solbjart. He was the hero who overcame great obstacles to win the hand of the incomparable Menglod.

SVIUR. A dwarf.

SVIVÖR. A giantess slain by Thor.

SVÖL. One of the icy rivers that arise from the spring Hvergelmir in Niflheim. See also ELIVAGAR.

SYLG. One of the icy rivers that arise from the spring Hvergelmir in Niflheim. See also ELIVAGAR.

SYN. One of the Asynjur. She is the doorkeeper who keeps out those who have no right to enter the hall.

SYR. A nickname Freyja sometimes uses when she seeks her wandering husband, Od.

T

TANNGNJOST. One of the two goats that pull Thor's chariot.

TANNGRISNIR. One of the two goats that pull Thor's chariot.

THAKKRAD. King Nidud's favorite thrall whom the king sent to fetch Bodvild when the king wished to ascertain if she was pregnant by Völund.

THEKK. A dwarf.

THEKK. A nickname of Odin.

THIR. The wife of Thrall and mother of the class of thralls.

Loki is carried off by Thjazi.

THJALFI. The son of Egil, brother of Röskva, and servant of Thor. He was the most swift-footed of men.

THJAZI. A giant; a son of Alvaldi, brother of Idi and Gang, and father of Skadi. Thjazi, in the guise of an eagle, kidnapped Idun and was slain by the Aesir when he pursued Loki and the rescued Idun into Asgard. His daughter, Skadi, was permitted to marry one of the gods for compensation. In addition, Odin cast Thjazi's eyes into the sky where they became two stars (Grimm, 1875-78, *Deutsche Mythologie*, suggested that they might be the Gemini).

THJOD. The home of King Hjalprek, where Regin fostered Sigurd.

THJODNUMA. One of the rivers that flow out of the spring Hvergelmir.

THJODRÖRIR. A dwarf who sang a runic charm before Delling's door—a song that brought strength to the Aesir, glory to the elves, and wisdom to Odin.

THJODVARA. One of the nine handmaidens of Menglod.

THJODVITNIR. Probably a nickname of Fenrir.

Thor and his Goat Cart.

THOR. A son of Odin and Jörd, brother of Meili, and father of Thrud (by Sif), Modi, and Magni (by Jarnsaxa). Thor is the strongest of all the gods and men. He drives a chariot pulled by two goats and owns three precious things: his hammer, Mjöllnir; his belt of strength; and his iron gloves—without which he cannot yield Mjöllnir. Thor is the implacable foe of giants and trolls—he is usually off in the East fighting them—and of the Midgard Serpent. He and the Serpent shall slay each other at Ragnarök.

THORIN. A dwarf.

THÖKK. Loki took this guise as a giantess when he refused to weep for Balder, thus condemning the god to remain with Hel.

THÖLL. One of the rivers that flow out of the spring Hvergelmir.

THRAIN. A dwarf. Presumably the same as Throin of the *Prose Edda*.

THRALL. The son of Rig and Edda; the progenitor of the class of thralls.

THRIDI. A nickname of Odin, and the one he assumed in occupying the highest seat of his three-tiered throne during the beguiling of King Gylfi. See also HAR and JAFNHAR.

THRIVALDI. A giant injured or slain by Thor.

THROIN. See THRAIN.

THROR. A dwarf.

THROR. A nickname of Odin.

THRUD. A valkyrie; the daughter of Thor and Sif.

THRUDGELMIR. A giant; the son of Aurgelmir and father of Bergelmir.

THRUDHEIM. The region of Asgard where Thor's hall, Bilskirnir, is situated.

THRUDVANGAR. Apparently equivalent to Thrudheim.

THRYM. The giant who stole Thor's hammer and held it as ransom for Freyja. He was deceived by Thor in a bridal gown and eventually slain by the god.

THRYMGJÖLL. The gate, made by three dwarves, that guards Menglod's hall.

THRYMHEIM. The mountain home of the giant Thjazi. It later passed to his daughter, Skadi.

THUND. The river that flows around Valhalla.

THUND. A nickname of Odin.

THURS. See JÖTUN.

THVITI. A huge stone used to drive the boulder Gjöll deep into the earth and thus anchor the wolf Fenrir's fetter.

THYN. One of the rivers that flow out of the spring Hvergelmir.

TROLL. In Viking-Age mythology, a term sometimes applied to hostile, ugly giants. In later folk tales, trolls took on other characteristics.

TVEGGI. A nickname of Odin.

TWILIGHT OF THE GODS. See RAGNARÖK, which is more correctly translated as Doom of the Gods.

TYR. The son of the giant Hymir, Tyr is the boldest and most courageous of the Aesir. He is invoked by warriors in battle. He is also very wise. Tyr has only one hand, having forfeited the other to bring about the binding of the great wolf Fenrir. At Ragnarök he and Garm, the hound of Hel, shall slay each other.

U

UD. One of the nine daughters of Aegir and Ran. She is called Unn in Hollander's translation of the *Poetic Edda.* She was said to possess an ice-cold stone (altar?) upon which sacred oaths were sworn.

UD. A river.

UD. A nickname of Odin.

ULFDALIR. The place where Völund and his brothers built their house.

ULFRUN. A giantess; one of the nine mothers of Heimdall.

ULFSJAR. A lake adjacent to Ulfdalir on the shores of which Völlund and his brothers "captured" their swan-maiden wives.

ULL. One of the Aesir; the son of Sif (by Aurvandil) and stepson of Thor. Ull is the best of bowmen and swiftest on skis and skates. He is a handsome warrior and is invoked by those engaging in single combat.

UNI. One of the nine dwarves who constructed the hall called Lyr, where Menglod dwelled.

UNN. See UD.

URD. The eldest of the three Norns who live in a beautiful hall near Urd's Well in Asgard. They determine the duration of each person's life. See also SKULD and VERDANDI.

URD'S WELL. A sacred well or spring that lies beneath the root of Yggdrasil in Asgard. Its water and clay are used by the three Norns who live nearby to daily sprinkle the tree and thus prevent its decay. This is the source of the dews that fall in the dales. The two swans that live in the spring are the progenitors of that race of birds. The Aesir hold their court of justice there.

URI. One of the nine dwarves who constructed the hall called Lyr, where Menglod dwelled.

The Norns at Urd's Well.

UTGARD. The term originally applied to the lands surrounding Midgard—between the mountains and the sea—where the giants live. Later it came to be restricted to the castle or stronghold of the giants that is situated in the middle of a plain in Jötunheim. Its ruler is Utgard-Loki.

UTGARD-LOKI. The ruler of the giants who dwell in Utgard. He is a powerful magician, a master of illusions. See SKRYMIR.

V

VADGELMIR. A river in Niflheim where oathbreakers are fated to wade.

VAFTHRUDNIR. A giant who engaged in a lore contest with Odin (in disguise) and lost his head in the process.

VAFUD. A nickname of Odin.

VAGASKER. A place frequented by Heimdall.

VAK. A nickname of Odin.

VALASKJALF. A dwelling in Asgard that is thatched with pure silver and belongs to Odin. Hollander indicated that this another name for Valhalla, but that hall is roofed with gold—not silver—and seems to serve a different purpose. Simek suggested that Valaskjalf might be associated with Odin's son Vali.

VALFADIR. A nickname of Odin.

VALGRIND. The gate of Valhalla.

VALHALLA. An enormous hall in Asgard whose roof is shingled with golden shields. It is one of two halls to which Odin assigns the battle-slain warriors who come to Asgard. It has 540 doors, from each of which 800 warriors will emerge at Ragnarök.

VALI. A son of Sigyn and Loki. The Aesir turned him into a wolf and caused him to tear his brother Nari apart so they could use Nari's intestines to bind Loki to three boulders.

VALI. The son of Odin and Rind. He is a daring fighter and a fine marksman. When only a day old he avenged Balder's death by slaying Höd.

VALI. The name used for the dwarf Nali in the *Prose Edda*.

VALKYRJAR (singular, VALKYRJA). The valkyries, women who are sent by Odin to the scene of every battle where they determine the outcome and choose who is to die. The valkyries also wait on table for the Einherjar in Valhalla.

VALLAND. A place where Odin went to stir up war. Its king was Kjar, whose daughter Olrun was a valkyrie and swanmaiden.

VALTAM. The one whom Odin, in the guise of Vegtam, claimed was his father when Odin raised a dead seeress to interpret Balder's nightmares.

VAN. The river formed from the saliva running from the mouth of the fettered wolf Fenrir.

VANADIS. A nickname of Freyja.

VANAHEIM. The realm of the Vanir.

VANIR (singular, VAN). The race of gods with whom the Aesir fought when the worlds were young. Njörd, Frey, and Freyja were the hostages they sent to the Aesir. The Vanir are frequently alluded to as being wise, and they chiefly are fertility gods.

VAR. One of the nine dwarves who constructed the hall called Lyr, where Menglod dwelled.

VAR. One of the Asynjur. She listens to vows (*varar*) pledged between men and women, and punishes any who break their vows.

VARKALD. Allegedly the father of Vindkald, a fictitious name Svipdag used in an attempt to deceive the giant Fjölsvid, who was guarding Menglod's abode.

VARTARI. The thong with which the dwarf Brokk sewed shut Loki's mouth after Loki managed to avoid forfeiting his head when he lost a wager with Brokk.

VASAD. A giant, the father of Vindljoni and grandfather of Vetr. He is grim and cold-hearted in temperament.

VE. A son of Bor and Bestla, and brother of Odin and Vili.

VEDRFÖLNIR. The hawk that sits between the eyes of the giant eagle (Hraesvelg) atop the ash tree Yggdrasil.

VEGDRASIL. One of the nine dwarves who constructed the hall called Lyr, where Menglod dwelled.

VEGSVIN. One of the rivers that flow out of the spring Hvergelmir.

VEGTAM. The name used by Odin when he raised a dead seeress to interpret Balder's nightmares.

VERATYR. A nickname of Odin.

VERDANDI. One of the three Norns who live in a beautiful hall near Urd's Well. They determine the duration of each person's life. See also SKULD and URD.

VERLAND. Presumably a nickname for Midgard. It was used by Odin on the occasion when, disguised as a ferryman, he refused to carry Thor over the water from Giantland to the land of men.

VESTRI. A dwarf; one of the four who hold up Ymir's skull (i.e., the sky). See also AUSTRI, NORDRI, and SUDRI.

VESTRSALIR. Rind's hall where she gave birth to Odin's son Vali, the Avenger.

VETR. A giant; the son of Vindljoni. He has his father's grim cold-hearted disposition.

VEUR. The nickname Thor used when he visited the giant Hymir.

VID. One of the icy rivers that arise from the spring Hvergelmir in Niflheim. See also ELIVAGAR.

VIDAR. The Silent God; the son of Odin and the giantess Grid, Vidar is almost as strong as Thor and is greatly relied upon by the other Aesir in difficult times. He wears thick shoes. He shall slay the wolf Fenrir after it swallows Odin at Ragnarök.

VIDBLAIN. The third level of the heavens, which lies above Andlang and in which the hall Gimle is situated. See also ANDLANG and ASGARD.

VIDBLINDI. A giant "who drew whales out of the sea like fishes."

VIDFINN. The father of Bil and Hjuki, the children who follow the moon through the heavens.

VIDI. Vidar's land in Asgard.

VIDOFNIR. Apparently a nickname of the cock Gullinkambi.

VIDOLF. The progenitor of all witches.

VIDUR. A nickname of Odin.

VIGG. A dwarf.

VIGRID. The plain upon which the final battle of Ragnarök will be fought. It measures 100 (probably the Viking-Age "long hundred," which was actually 120) leagues wide in each direction.

VILI. A son of Bor and Bestla, and brother of Odin and Ve.

VILMEID. The progenitor of all wizards.

VIMUR. A river Thor forded on his journey to Geirrödagard.

VIN. One of the rivers that flow out of the spring Hvergelmir.

VINA. One of the rivers that flow out of the spring Hvergelmir.

VINDALF. A dwarf.

VINDHEIM. Heaven, the home of the gods. Presumably this is the same as Asgard. However, see also ANDLANG and VIDBLAIN.

VINDKALD. The fictitious name Svipdag used in an attempt to deceive the giant Fjölsvid, who was guarding Menglod's abode.

VINDLER. A nickname of Heimdall.

VINDLJONI. A giant. The grim and cold-hearted son of Vasad, and father of Vetr.

VINDSVAL. A nickname of Vindljoni.

VINGNIR. A foster son (?) of Thor.

VINGOLF. One of the two halls (the other is Valhalla) to which Odin assigns the battle-slain warriors who come to Asgard. This also is the name of the hall in

Asgard that serves as a sanctuary for the goddesses. It is not clear if this name refers to one hall or two.

VINGTHOR. A nickname of Thor.

VIRVIR. One of the dwarves in Dvalin's band, which left the rocks to settle on a sandy plain.

VIT. A dwarf.

VOND. A river that flows through Midgard and thence to Hel's realm.

VÖLUND. A master smith; the brother of Egil and Slagfid, and husband of the valkyrie Hervor. They lived in Ulfdalir. When, in the ninth year, Hervor and her sister valkyries flew off through Myrkvid to the wars, Völund remained in Ulfdalir while his brothers sought their wives. The smith was hamstrung by King Nidud to force him to labor for the king, and for this treatment Völund took a fearful revenge upon the king and his family. The king addressed Völund as "elflord," so presumably the smith is an elf.

W

WEIRD OF THE GODS. See RAGNARÖK.

WORLD ASH. See YGGDRASIL.

WORLD TREE. See YGGDRASIL.

Y

YDALIR. That part of Asgard where Ull has his hall.

YGG. A nickname of Odin.

YGGDRASIL. The great ash tree whose limbs spread over all the Nine Worlds. It has three great roots: one among the Aesir; one among the Frost Giants where Ginnungagap once lay; and one in Niflheim. Beneath the root in Asgard lies the sacred Well of Urd, beneath that in Jötunheim is Mimir's Well, and beneath that in Niflheim is the great spring Hvergelmir.

YLG. One of the icy rivers that arise from the spring Hvergelmir in Niflheim. See also ELIVAGAR.

YMIR. The oldest being and progenitor of the race of Frost Giants, who called him Aurgelmir. He formed in Ginnungagap from the drops of venomous meltwater that resulted from the frost out of Niflheim being melted by the heat from Muspellheim.

YNGVI. One of the dwarves in Dvalin's band, which left the rocks to settle on a sandy plain.

YNGVI. A nickname of Frey.

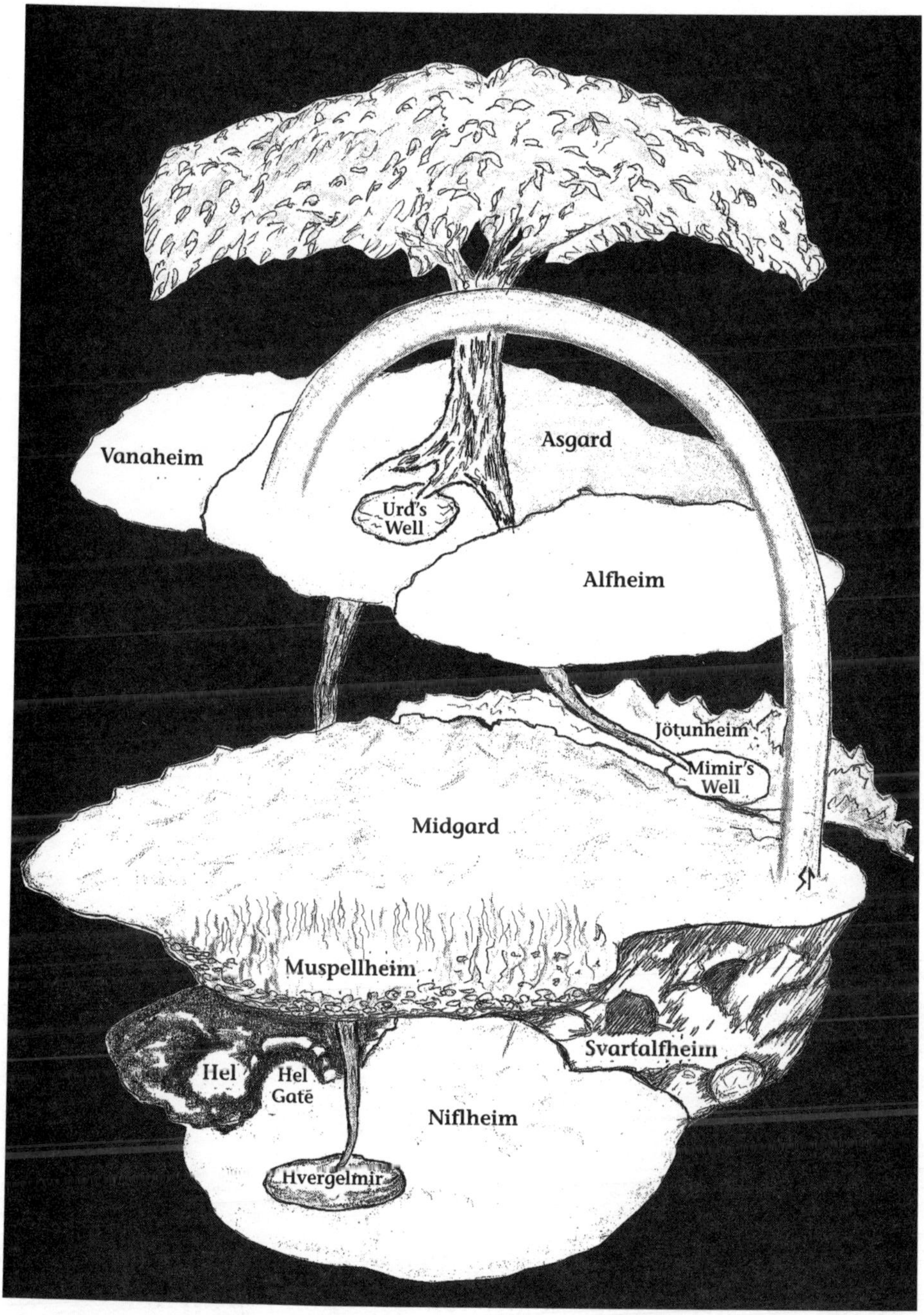

Yggdrasil, the World Tree, unites the Nine Worlds.

Photo opposite page: "Dag" and Sharon Rossman on Onstad farm, Volbufjord, Øystre Slidre, Valdres. Strande farm (the buildings across the lake behind them) was the last one in Norway to belong to his direct ancestors before it was sold when they came to America in 1864. His great-great grandmother lived there; her husband was from Onstad farm.

About "Dag" and Sharon Rossman

Known for his passionate retellings of Norse myths and Viking tales, "Dag" Rossman is a gifted storyteller who shares a passion for Norse mythology with his wife Sharon, an artist. "Dag" has had a dozen short stories published—most of them set in the Nine Worlds of Norse mythology, and several of them illustrated by Sharon. The two of them co-authored ***Valhalla in America: Norse Myths in Wood at Rock Island State Park, Wisconsin*** (1999, Jackson Harbor Press, Washington Island, WI). Dag's storytelling skills are in great demand at folk festivals, heritage camps, and other Scandinavian events. Five of his storytelling collections have been released by Skandisk, Inc. on audiocassette (available in Scandinavian gift stores nationwide, or by calling 1-800-468-2424).

"Dag" was a biology professor at Louisiana State University for more than 35 years, while Sharon was a special education teacher in the local school system. They now live in Decorah, Iowa, where they have served as guest curators for the Vesterheim Norwegian-American Museum's major exhibition, "Echoes of Odin: Norse Mythology in Scandinavia and America."

DRENGSKAPUR

HEROIC CODE OF THE VIKING AGE

sannferdighet ("truthfulness")
— always be honest

hjelpsomhet ("helpfulness")
— aid those in need

trofasthet ("loyalty")
— be true to those who are true to you

sjelestyrke ("fortitude")
— hang in there when life gets tough

tapperhet ("courage")
— face your fears

selvrespekt ("self-respect")
— do nothing to harm your integrity or good name

selvbestemmelse ("self-determination")
— take charge of your own life

selvstyre ("self-restraint")
— control your behavior

selvstendighet ("self-reliance")
— don't ask others to do for you what you can do for yourself